How My Disastrous Teenage Love Life Will Get You An INTERNSHIP

BY ANDREW OSAYEMI

How My Disastrous Teenage Love Life Will Get You An Internship by Andrew Osayemi. Published by Seun Boy Publishing, London

ABOUT THE AUTHOR

Andrew Osayemi is a Netflix TV show creator, ex-financial markets trader and a graduate recruitment expert who has helped thousands of high-potential student get top internships and graduate jobs.

Andrew has worked as a graduate recruitment specialist for the award-winning graduate diversity recruitment firm, Rare Recruitment; working with global firms such as Deutsche Bank, JP Morgan, Morgan Stanley, UBS, KPMG, Bain, BCG, McKinsey, Oliver Wyman, WPP, BP, FHF London and many more! He understands interviews and how to impress interviewers inside out, and he can't wait to share his secrets to help you get your dream job.

Andrew started his career working for RBS as a Forward FX Trader in London and New York. At 27, he left RBS and founded an international TV production company, MTA Productions. MTA enjoyed huge success in creating TV shows which were sold to over 20 countries and watched by millions. The hit shows included *Meet the Adebanjos* (which ran for 3 seasons/50 episodes and is currently airing on Netflix) and *The T Boy Show*, which ran for 2 seasons/23 episodes.

EXTRA RESOURCES

Follow me on LinkedIn to hear more of my crazy stories and to get access to my exclusive interview help webinars https://www.linkedin.com/in/andrew-osayemi/

DEDICATION

To my beautiful wife, for putting up with me all these years and for saying yes when I asked her to dance all those years ago. To my son; I hope you use these secrets when you grow up. To my family; thank you for always having my back. To Kay; thank you for sharing all these secrets with me, which I have used to achieve great success throughout my life. To the reader; thank you for reading and making this book worthwhile.

Contents

INTRODUCTION

I remember back when I was 14 years old. I had recently moved from living in Peckham, South East London (which back then was a concrete jungle filled with social housing, where as a young guy you had to watch your back at all times) to an area in deeper South London that my parents considered safer — South Norwood.

My parents had one specific dream for me: to do well at school so that I could improve my social setting in life and avoid the trap that many people I grew up with ended up in — selling drugs and winding up in prison.

I, however, had a different dream than my parents. I had one dream that I was completely obsessed with, a dream that kept me up all night and daydreaming throughout the day. It was the dream of getting a girlfriend!! But I was clueless, I didn't know where to find one or what to do to get one. I went to a mixed school but a school that only started accepting girls the year I joined, so there weren't yet many girls in the school. Also, all the girls in the school seemed to like the older boys. The only other place I knew that had girls was the church I went to with my parents on Sundays. But I had known all the girls there since I was like 5, so they were all like sisters to me. What was I to DO?!!

I had a good friend called Kay, who just seemed to attract girls. He was like a lady magnet; I didn't know how he did it. He was always telling me stories about the girls he met and how they liked him. And these were girls I could only dream about in my wildest dreams. Girls our age and older!!

So, one day I asked him while we were chilling in McDonald's — what was his secret? Where did he find all these girls? Because I didn't know any place where girls hung out. He said he would take me to a place on Saturday. My parents weren't going to allow me to go on a girlfriend mission all day on Saturday when I had studying to do. In fact, both my parents were highly religious, so even mentioning 'girlfriend' in our house was not allowed. So that Saturday I told my mom and dad that I was going out to study in the library. But, in fact, I met up with Kay in Peckham and we jumped on the Number 12 bus, which Kay said would take us to a place of milk and honey — filled with girls. Kay took me to a place called Oxford Street, the most popular shopping street in London, where all the high-end fashion brands had their flagship shops. The street was about one mile long, and on this street were so many girls — more than I had ever seen in my life. All different shapes and sizes! I was in heaven!!!

I locked eyes with one particular girl, and she locked eyes with me.

"Kay, she is beautiful — like an Angel!" I said.

Kay grinned and said to me, "Go and try to say hello and talk to her then."

"Right now?" I stuttered, "On this busy street, in front of all these thousands of people?"

"Yes, why not?" Kay said. "Just go and introduce yourself — how do you think I get as many girls as I do? I simply go up to girls and start having a conversation."

I had never done anything like this, but if Kay the Lady Magnet said this is what he did to get girls, who was I to argue? I had to follow in his footsteps if I wanted to succeed.

So, I slowly walked over to the girl, who was standing outside Topshop, lighty tapped her on her shoulder and said, "Hi, my name is Andrew and I would like you to be my girlfriend."

I looked back at Kay, who was across the street, and grinned a cheesy grin. Kay gave me the thumbs up!

She also was grinning. *Wow, this actually works,* I thought. I repeated my opening statement.

"Hi, my name is Andrew and I would like you to be my girlfriend."

This time she burst out laughing and said, "Are you serious"?

"Yes, I am — would you like to be my girlfriend?"

She then called over her friends and told them what I had said, and they burst out laughing. Her friends called other friends and *they* burst out laughing. Before you knew it, there was a crowd of people, all laughing.

The girl then noticed I was still standing there and said to me in front of everyone, "The answer is NO NO NO, fool. Now get out of my face!" and everyone laughed so hard they were crying.

Feeling like such an idiot, I walked across the road to Kay. "What happened, bro?" he said. When I explained what happened, he was like, "Oh no! All I said to you was to introduce yourself; not *propose* to her."

I started to think that maybe this was a bad idea. I felt so embarrassed. I said to Kay, "Bro, let's just go home. I don't think this is for me." Kay, sensing my spirit had been crushed, said something to me which has stuck with me all my life. He said, "Bro, don't focus on 'No'. Focus on earning your 'Yes!'

"How I'm I going to start getting girls to say yes to me?" I exclaimed. "Didn't you see the reaction of the girls? I simply don't have it."

He said, "Don't worry. I'm going to teach you how to earn your yes and get a girlfriend!!!"

And over the next year, Kay taught me all his secrets of how he got girls to like him.

When I got to university, I arrived knowing that my number one goal was to get a great job at the end of my studies. But the same thing happened with this as when I first started, years ago, looking for a girlfriend. Every interview I went for I was rejected, time after time. I remember pouring out my frustrations to Kay on the phone. He told me, "Andrew, why don't you do the same things I taught you while helping you to get the girls back in the day, and use the same techniques to do well in interviews?"

"But Kay, getting a girlfriend and a job are two completely different things."

He replied, "Trust me, they are the same. It's all about getting someone to like you and decide you are worth investing in."

So, I started to use his secret techniques and it actually began to work. I started not getting rejected in the first round and making it to the final round. I started to get internships and finally ended up getting a full time analyst job as a trader in the investment division of a major UK Bank. I also used the same techniques Kay taught me to start up my TV production business when I left banking, which led to me ultimately creating a TV series that is now on Netflix.

So, this book is about sharing everything Kay taught me to help me get a girlfriend — to help you get a top internship and ultimately your dream job! This book will also help give you the tools to achieve any goal you have in life!

Are you ready to learn the secrets?

CHAPTER ONE

DO YOUR RESEARCH

A GIRL CALLED SUZANNE

I remember when I was fifteen, there was a particular girl that lived across the road from my parents' house; every guy I knew in the area fancied her. Her name was Suzanne, and she was absolutely stunning in every way. An amazing personality, supermodel looks, and she had a smile that would make you feel like you were the most special person in the world. I would wait at my window for hours for a chance to see her leave her house.

But she was off-limits. She was off-limits because the only type of guys that she seemed to go for were much older guys, even though she was the same age as I was. Guys that looked like they worked out in the gym 24/7 and got their hair cut every three days. Guys who would pull up to her house in a drop-top Audi TT fresh from the car wash. You know, guys who made it so guys like me didn't have a chance.

One hot day in the summer holidays, my friend Kay came round to visit, and I told him about Suzanne. Kay's reaction was, "Damn, I gotta see what the hype is all about!" So, we sat outside my house, just waiting to see if we could catch a glimpse of her as she came home. We waited for hours until eventually we saw her slowly walking to her house.

"Hi, Suzanne!" I shouted across the road casually, trying to look like we were just chilling, watching cars go by instead of just waiting for her. She smiled, waved at us and went into her house.

I turned to Kay and his mouth was wide open, and his jaw was almost at the floor. He had been smitten. "Damn, she is sooo fiiine," he exclaimed. "Andrew, you weren't lying one bit. In fact, she is even finer than how you described her. Oh, my days! That's my next girlfriend."

I fell about, laughing at the audacity of Kay thinking they could become boyfriend and girlfriend. "Kay, I know you're Mr Ladies' Man, but you don't have a chance." I giggled uncontrollably. "You're not in her league. You're not even old enough to drive. All the guys she goes with are ballers!"

Kay glared at me defiantly. "Watch me — I bet you I can do it."

He then proceeded to ask me so many questions about her. What is her favourite food to eat, favourite musical artists, favourite trainers, fashion designer? When he exhausted all his questions on me, he befriended some of Suzanne's friends and found out even more about Suzanne.

A few weeks later, Suzanne and her friends invited us to hang out with them at the park. While most of us were water fighting, playing rounders or chilling, listening to music, Suzanne and Kay sat under a tree talking for hours. Their talks continued throughout the summer, when Kay would come every day and just hang out on our street. Our group used to find someone whose parents were at work and just hang out at their house. At nights, Kay and Suzanne would spend hours on the phone, talking way into the early morning. By the end of the summer, they were boyfriend and girlfriend.

When I asked Kay what was his secret, and how did he manage to convince her to be his girlfriend when many others had tried and failed, he filled me in: "Andrew remember all those questions I was asking you about her? Well, that was me doing my research. I would then go and learn about all the things I found out she was interested in so that when we talked, we had a lot to talk about. Women love men who are interested in what they are interested in, so I became an expert! That's how we became so close, and I let my charm do the rest of the work."

He ended with this gem: "Andrew, if you want to start improving your chances for getting girls, you have to research them more to find out what they are into!"

And that's just the thing you need to do when it comes to an internship interview. You need to research everything about the internship you want to try for. That's the most important thing! You need to do your research.

This section will give you some tips on how to research your dream internship!

ACTION POINT – USE GOOGLE, IT'S FREE!

People do internships because they want to find out if this is the right job for them before they apply full time or to get more experience in an industry they ultimately want to get into. So knowing everything about the industry and your dream job is so important.

How well do you know your dream job? Is it a job someone told you would be good for you, or did you hear that it offered a good salary? You gotta be like Kay and do your research.

Task: Can you answer all the questions below? If you can't, you'd better hit Google immediately and start doing your research.

- Who are the top 10 firms in the industry you are looking to apply to?
- What makes each firm stand out from the other?
- Which firms offer internships?
- Which firms will offer a full time offer if you impress during an internship?
- How long are the internships for?
- When do the internships take place?
- When is the opening and closing application window for internships?
- What are the minimum eligibility requirements?
- How much will you be paid per week during the internship?
- What is the application and interview process like?
- What is a typical full-time starting salary?

MAMA! I MADE IT!

My Mama was so proud of me. She couldn't believe it — her son was working in investment banking (even though she didn't really understand what the investment banking industry was). You see, my parents were immigrants who came from Nigeria as university students with nothing except their dreams. Due to prejudice and discrimination, many of their dreams didn't work out as they would have liked. So, their major goal became making sure their British-born children made it in life. So, my working in investment banking was a source of great pride for them and elevated their status among their friends.

So, you can imagine how my mum felt when after five years of me working in investment banking, which included a two-year stint working in New York, I told her I was leaving the industry to become a TV producer. She was stunned: *Are you OK? Should I take you to my pastor to pray for you? Who has brainwashed my son?*

My Dad had similar concerns. You see, I had suddenly gotten fired because by my return to London from New York the company had suffered losses, and it didn't have the same headcount as it used to — I had to go. So, my Dad thought my 'poor judgement' was the effect of me being fired, and that's why I was making this decision. He was sort of correct. The firing made me really consider what I wanted to achieve in my life.

I remember hearing a saying around that time: *When you're on your death bed, what would you want to have achieved in your life?* I thought I would have liked to have impacted as many people as possible and also pursued the things I loved. You see, as I was growing up, I loved reading books. I was raised in a house where we didn't have a TV. Throughout my childhood and teenage years, the only way I could get any entertainment was to read books. I was the person who took out the maximum number of books from the library (9) and returned them at the end of the week because I had read all of them! Long before Netflix and Chill, I was doing Reading and Chilling!

So, I decided I wanted to produce stories and bring some of my ideas to life. I joined forces with a family friend, Debra, and set up a TV production company. I had so much enthusiasm and energy, and with that energy – with that enthusiasm – I was able to raise over a hundred thousand pounds to co-create the first season of a TV show we called *Meet the Adebanjos*. It was about a British-Nigerian family living in London. The concept involved the differences between kids born in the UK and their Nigerian parents. It was in part based on my background and that of my co-creator, Debra, as we both grew up in households where the contrast between the cultures of the parents and kids caused so much comedy. We and our investors thought we were onto a winner.

For a year we pitched to all the mainstream broadcasters, and they said they wouldn't buy a show that had been already produced. Also, they didn't like the concept! We hadn't done our research, we had spent £100K and we were screwed!!

Luckily, just as we were running out of options it was suggested there would be a massive market for our show in Africa. That made sense to us because our show was about an African family living in the UK. So, we took our last bit of money and booked a trip to the biggest African TV conference; called Discop, it was taking place in Ghana that year. At that conference, you could network with TV buyers from TV stations across Africa and negotiate deals.

The reaction from every TV station that visited our viewing booth was incredible. They laughed so much at our trailer and exclaimed, "Wow – we have never seen this before. This is unique and different! We love it!!!!"

Debra and I gave each other looks like, "YES – our prayers are going to be answered." All our sacrifices, time away from partners, racking up credit card bills, hardly getting any sleep — this was the moment our lives were going to be turned around.

But no one wanted to discuss money or place an order. We started to get worried.

On the last day, Debra was able to set up a meeting with one of the biggest buyers of TV content in the region. He came to meet us with two assistants. I was thinking, *Wow, this man must have loads of money to have two assistants!*

We got down to negotiating how much he wanted to pay to licence our first season (a TV station pays you a fee for the right to air/licence your show for a length of time — typically a year). The buyer kicked off negotiations by saying he would pay us 200,000 per episode. Debra and I were in shock! 200,000 per episode. That was more for one episode than it cost to make the whole series (we had spent 100,000 for seven episodes). That meant we were getting 7 x 200,000 which meant 1.4 million! We would be making 1.3 million profit!!

I started to think to myself: *Mama, I told you I could make something from this TV stuff!* I started thinking about how I was going to spend the money. Then I remembered: this is a negotiation, and you don't just accept the first offer. I countered almost sheepishly, "We can't do 200,000 per episode. We can only do it for 300,000 per episode." Debra was looking at me like *What the hell are you doing? Don't mess this up – we need to take the deal, fool!*

The buyer came back with, "Oh, so you are a negotiator. I can only go up to 250,000."

I said *250,000? We have a deal!* and he said *Done!* 250,000 an episode was 1.75 million. Debra looked at me as if she wanted to say, *We're rich!!!* She then asked, "Is that in dollars or pounds?" They started to laugh and didn't let up for at least two minutes. When they finished laughing, they said, "No, that's in Nigerian naira."

The blood left our faces. Nigerian naira has a high exchange rate. At the time of writing this book, it's 500 naira to 1 pound. So, 250,000 naira was actually 500 pounds. Instead of 1.75 million pounds, we were being offered only £3500.

When they saw our dejected faces, they started to laugh again. *You thought we were talking in pounds or dollars.* When they finally stopped laughing, they asked us if, before coming to the conference, we had done any research into what African TV stations pay for brand new shows? We sheepishly shook our heads and said we based our assumptions on UK TV licencing deals.

We didn't do our research! We had made assumptions instead of actually doing the work and researching! That mistake ended up costing us many years of trying to figure out a new business model. We'd created a company based on a business model in which we would be getting paid far more than what we were initially offered. We didn't do our research. And if you don't do your research, it will cause you this sort of pain. It will cause you rejections. It will cause you a lot of failure and you won't understand why.

It's important. Do your research.

ACTION POINT – RESEARCH THE INDUSTRY

You need to know everything about an industry before you go into it. Imagine if a stranger asked you to go into business with them. You would probably do as much research as possible on that person, right? You need to do the same with the industry of your prospective job. Here are some considerations you should be researching:

- Who are the top 10 firms in the industry?
- What are the 10 biggest trends in the industry? What is your solution to the trends?
- What are the 10 biggest challenges the industry is facing?
- What is the work culture like in the industry?

You also need to stay on top of industry news day-to-day so that you keep up to date with your knowledge base. You can stay up to date the following ways:

- Google news alerts – Set up Google news keyword alerts for names of firms you want to work at or topics relevant to your industry.
- Podcasts – This is my favourite. Every time I want to study a topic I know nothing about, I consume all the top podcasts on the topic. This allows me to get up to speed very quickly.
- Forums – Join industry forums and read each day about the topics that affect the industry.
- News websites – Read industry websites daily.

- LinkedIn – Follow the industry thought leaders on LinkedIn.

MY FIRST INVESTMENT BANKING INTERVIEW

I remember my first major interview, with one of the world's biggest investment banks, Goldman Sachs, in my first year at university. It was for an internship opportunity and I had gotten to the first-round interview.

I thought I would ace this interview because I had some work experience at my local retail bank when I was eighteen; where regular people came in and you sorted out their money issues. In the branch where I had worked, I had experienced so many different types of customers I felt this put me at an advantage above everyone else who was applying for the internship.

On the day of the interview, I made sure I had my best church suit ironed and ready to go. My shoes were so shiny you could see my reflection in them, and my haircut was so fresh I looked like the models you see in the window of barbershops! I looked the part!

I travelled up to central London, marvelling at all the impressive buildings and thinking that very soon I would be working in these buildings. I turned up 30 minutes early, just as I had been advised to by my parents. The reception was an impressive place and I began to feel nervous.

You're not cut out to work in a place like this, a voice in my head whispered to me. *Who do you think you are fooling?* another voice growled. *Maybe if you left now no one would notice.* I started to get more and more uncomfortable, but I was saved by someone from HR who came down and told me I had done well for having come down, and was I ready for the maths test?

Maths test? I didn't know there was any maths test. Before I had a chance to reply, I was bundled into a room and set down in front of a test paper. "You have 30 minutes," the lady said. I asked if she had any spare calculators. The woman looked at me strangely. "No calculators are allowed. But you can use the extra paper to help you out."

The maths test was tough; made even tougher by the fact that I had not practised mental maths in many years. I couldn't even finish half the test, and it was multiple-choice!!

I then went into an interview with two senior people who asked me many questions about investment banking. I told them everything I had researched about banking. Before I had even talked for 30 seconds, one of the interviewers stopped me.

"I think you are telling us about retail banking. Do you know the difference between retail banking and investment banking? We are an investment bank and not a retail bank."

I replied, "I never heard of a difference between retail banking and investment banking. All I know is banking. Isn't it all the same? Current accounts and savings accounts?"

The two senior people looked at each other in disbelief because I didn't have a clue that investment banking was different from regular High Street banking. In all fairness, I should have known better, but I hadn't done the proper research into the firm and the industry. I went with what I thought I knew, and that cost me big time!!

I think my interview was the shortest interview in history. It only lasted two minutes before I was sent on my merry way! And I was not surprised I didn't get a call-back for the second round.

I had failed to do proper research. I took what I knew for granted and hadn't bothered to put in the work required. After that disastrous interview, I vowed never again to show up at an interview without doing my research.

ACTION POINT – RESEARCH THE INTERVIEW STYLE AND THE TYPES OF QUESTIONS ASKED

Do you know the type of questions that will be asked during the internship interview you're applying for? Do you know the style the questions will take (e.g., competency, strength-based, technical, case interviews and many other types)? Don't be fooled by thinking all internships ask the same type of interview questions in the same style. Different firms and different internships interview in different ways.

How to research interview styles/questions —

1. Type "What is the interview style of X internship" and "What are the typical interview questions of X internship" in Google (or any search engine).
2. This should take you to interview forums appropriate to your internship, where previous intern applicants discuss their interview experiences.
3. Write down all the information about the style of interview and the questions asked.
4. Start working on improving your knowledge, so you can answer all the questions expertly.
5. Also check to see if there are any tests given during the application/interview, and research training sites to help you prepare.

CORNERED AT A WEDDING!

I was recently at a wedding, having a fantastic time, when a young lady cornered me near the buffet table. She said, "Hi, my name is Michelle. I follow you on LinkedIn. Can you give me some advice, as I have been struggling to get my dream job?"

In my head I was thinking, *Damn, I can't even go out to enjoy myself without having to do work.* Also, I was thinking to myself that I just got to the front of the buffet queue and I really want to eat my food. But I could see the sincerity in Michelle's eyes, and I told her to come back and find me in twenty minutes, after I had finished my food. In 19 minutes and 59 seconds, Michelle was back!

Before answering her question, I asked her a few questions of my own just to see if she had a personality and if she would come across as interesting and competent in an interview. That is normally 60% of what is required at an interview, as the interviewer wants to know if they can work with you as well as whether you have the right skills for the role.

Michelle passed with flying colours. She was engaging and clearly was passionate for the graduate role she wanted to get — as an accountant at a big firm.

I told her, "Wow, I don't see why you should have any problem at an interview. You don't need my help."

She replied, "That's the problem, Andrew, I can't even get an interview."

"That must be a screening issue," I replied.

Each firm has different screening processes to narrow down the number of applications they have to review. Some use qualifications, some use subjects you have studied, some use experience. Whatever it is, this is something you need to research so you can position yourself or know what you need to add to your CV.

I suggested she research the grade requirements. She said "I already have. My A-Level grades are above the minimum requirement."

I said, "Do you know that some top accountancy firms can look as far back as GCSE grades?" She went away and did some research.

The next day, she called me up told me she found her GCSE maths grade was below the minimum they would allow for the job, which meant that her application was being rejected automatically at the first stage. She was distraught, as she really wanted to have an accountancy job.

I told her there was no point being distraught. It was time for her to FIGHT BACK. I told her to STOP applying for any more jobs. I suggested she focus on retaking GCSE maths and then apply once she got the minimum grade. She retook her GCSE maths within 6 months, got the top grade and is now working as an accountant.

You have to do your research!!!

ACTION POINT – RESEARCH THE QUALIFICATIONS

One key research people often forget to do is to look into the qualifications, technical and eligibility requirements that are needed for the internship role they are applying to. What a lot of people don't understand or realise is that, in the first screening process of an internship application, many firms use minimum qualifications/technical/eligibility requirements criteria to narrow the number of students they have to review. If they did not do this, they would be overwhelmed with applications. The minimum requirement could be a type of degree you have to be doing, a minimum grade you must have reached, relevant work experience, specific key skills etc. Some firms go back as far as your high school grades. Have you checked if you have the right qualifications or technical requirements for your dream internship?

How to Check Requirements —

- Go to internship websites and check for minimum qualification requirements and technical requirements.
- Go to internship forums to double-check if there is a minimum unofficial requirement, such as A-Level or GCSE grades.
- Don't forget to check the university year eligibility requirement. Some internships only allow students in their penultimate years. Other internships are more flexible.

If You Don't Have the Minimum Requirements —

- If you don't meet the internship's minimum requirements, research courses you can do that can give you the necessary qualifications/technical requirements needed.

- Look for firms which uses a different screening criteria which you would qualify for their internship programme. Not all firms look at grades.
- Attend as many career networking events as possible and sell yourself directly to the recruiters making sure you explain to them the issue regarding the minimum requirements. If you impress the recruiter or business representative they can bypass the minimum requirements just for you.

GOING CLUBBING AT SEVENTEEN!

When I was seventeen, the highlight of the weekend was going clubbing with my friends. We liked to attend clubs with a squad of at least 6 to 8 friends, made up of Kay and my childhood friends who all grew up in South East London. We would excitedly talk about the best club to go to. My cousin John, who was two years older, always knew the best spots. We would make sure our clothes were freshly ironed and our hair was looking groomed; I would make sure I had a lie or an excuse prepared for my parents, so they'd let me out. (Normally I would be doing all-night studying at a friend's house. 😊) We would then all bundle up, squeeze ourselves into John's car and head towards the West End to the latest happening club.

When we first started clubbing, we made one fatal mistake. We would look at the time on the flyers, say 10 pm – 4 am, and try to time our arrival to when the club would be the liveliest. This was normally around 1 am. We would get to the club and there would be a line around the block. We would stand in the line for hours and, when we got to the front, they would say either the club was full or they couldn't accept so many guys into the club. The rule in our squad was: all of us in or none of us in. So, if we all couldn't get in, we would decide to find another club, which normally wasn't as good as the club we first wanted to get into.

One day I asked a bouncer how we could avoid the queues and guarantee we always get in. He said to make sure we got there when the club opened. So, we changed our strategy to get to the clubs when they opened, and we no longer had issues about getting in. In fact, because we were so early, we almost always qualified for some special promotion — half price for everyone before X time because they wanted to get people into the club to get the party started. The only downside is that we had to wait for two hours before the club got lively; we had no money, so we looked broke asking for free water at the bar and pretending it was gin and tonic!

The same kind of thing happens with many internships and graduate jobs. They hire on a rolling basis, which means if you don't apply within the first two weeks of the application opening you might miss out. If you submit your application just before the deadline, they most likely will have already hired everyone and you won't be able to get an internship!

Don't delay, make sure you apply as soon as the internship opens for applications!

ACTION POINT – RESEARCH THE TIME PERIOD FOR APPLICATIONS

You don't want to miss an opportunity because you didn't know when deadlines closed. Here's how not to miss deadlines —

1. Always check the internship description to find out the opening date and closing date for applications.
2. Try to apply within 2 weeks of the opening date.
3. Always try to find out whether the firm reviews applications on a rolling basis or all at once after the deadline.
4. Create a spreadsheet that lists all the above points for all the firms you want to apply to.
5. When in doubt, always apply early!

PITCHING TO OTHER TV PRODUCTION COMPANIES

I remember one particular day, Debra and I were going to a meeting pitch with another TV production company, right in the beginning when we first had the idea of making *Meet the Adebanjos*. This production company was one of the biggest in the UK and had made many mainstream hits; we wanted to pitch them on coming on board to co-produce the show with us.

The offices of the production company were on the other side of town, so we had to take a train to get there. I met Debra at the station, and she was looking at me funny. But I didn't think too much of it. I was dressed very smart in a grey pin-striped suit. I had on a fresh white shirt with a crisp red tie. This was a big deal for us, and I wanted to impress. Debra, on the other hand, came dressed casually in jeans and a jumper. I was going to tell her when we finished the meeting that next time she should arrive more dressed up.

But when we got to the production company meeting, I saw that they were all dressed like Debra and they were also looking at me a bit funny.

During the meeting they were using lots of buzzwords about the creative industry; words I didn't know. I kept asking them to explain what they meant by the buzzwords as I was very confused. Debra gave me a look of *You better nod your head and pretend you know what they are talking about.*

We finished the meeting, shook hands and said our goodbyes. As we were walking back to the train station I said to Debra, "I think that went well."

"They're never going to work with us," Debra scowled.

"Why?"

"Because you look like a bloody accountant. You look like you have nothing to do with TV production. You looked lost when they spoke in industry jargon. You do not fit the part. Andrew, you gotta fix up!"

I was devastated because I came from a background in banking, where you were told to dress smart — look the best, look very sharp, especially if you are going for a meeting with important clients. But then I realised I was not conforming to the ways the creative industry dresses. I hadn't done my research. I came across as way too stiff. I made people feel uncomfortable. Creative people don't like people who dress like accountants. Debra told me I have to dress more creatively to make people believe I'm part of the creative industry.

I took this on board. The next day I went straight to H&M and Topshop and bought turtleneck jumpers, Chelsea Boots, big glasses. I grew my hair. I also started to listen to TV industry podcasts so that I could learn the jargon and language of the TV industry. And before you know it, when I went to these TV production company meetings or creative pitches in general, I looked the part and sounded the part; people started to take Debra and me more seriously.

To convince someone you are hireable, you must know the industry inside out. You need to know the way people dress, the way people speak, the way people think. Do your research.

ACTION POINT — RESEARCH THE DRESS CODE AND THE BUZZWORDS

Dress and Vocabulary Checklist —

- Research if the job requires a business smart, smart or casual dress code — how smart and how casual is important.
- Research what dress code is appropriate for interviews (some casual firms still expect you to dress smart at interviews).
- Create a vision board of the style of dresser you want to be at work. Start shopping to build up your wardrobe.
- Learn the different buzzwords and language of your industry by watching YouTube videos and listening to podcasts. If there is anything you don't understand, go and do further research.

SHE WANTS TO DATE A THUG!

Sometimes when you do your research you find out that what you think of as your dream job is not all you thought it was.

I remember when I was young, and I was attracted to this girl. I really liked her, so I used the same technique Kay taught me about doing as much research as possible to try to figure out what type of boy she might like. The plan was that once I found out her type, I was determined to be that type of boy.

So, I found out through the grapevine she likes thugs. I thought, *Okay, I'm gonna be a thug.* So, I started to wear the type of clothes that the thugged-out guys she liked wore. I went to the barber and changed my hairstyle. I changed my type of walk, my type of swagger. And I noticed she started liking me more and more. So, I kept up the act. Then one day there was a guy that she had a disagreement with, and she said, "Andrew, you're a thug. Why don't you go and fight the guy for me?" And that's when I realised — I don't want to be a thug anymore. That's not me. And I dropped the act and stopped pretending!

Once you do your research, if you find the job is not for you, don't do it! Just go and do something else that is more aligned with your skill set. Never follow the crowd and bow to peer pressure. Don't be going into something that's not you. Once you've done that research and you find out it's not for you, it's not worth throwing all your energy into it. It's simply not worth it!

I'm not saying you shouldn't go into a job that will push you and is hard. I'm saying that if you find that your skill set doesn't fit into the job or that it's a job you will enjoy, look for a job that fits your skillset better.

I remember my parents telling me to consider becoming a doctor. I did some research and saw you have to be around sick people and work in a hospital for long hours each day, and I thought to myself, *I get a bit light-headed when I'm in a hospital. I don't think I could do it day after day.* I decided my skill set and interest didn't align with that job, so it was time to look at something else! Don't follow the crowd. Do your research!

ACTION POINT – IS THIS JOB FOR YOU?

Task: Write down all the things you want from a job. Does your job tick enough of the boxes that you want it to? Sometimes, you may be willing to take a job that doesn't tick all your boxes if it pays well or provides you with good benefits. But just know that sometime in the future you could be looking to move on to something else or you will be unhappy. It's OK to take some short-term pain for long-term gain, but just be sure you know in the beginning what you are getting yourself into. You will always move up faster in a job you love than you will in a job you hate.

DO YOUR RESEARCH!

CHAPTER TWO

YOU'VE GOT TO BE MORE INTERESTING

MY TEENAGE CRUSH

I remember when I was around eighteen there was a girl I really, really liked called Clare. She was part of the same friendship group I belonged to and I had always fancied her. There was something about her that just spoke "wifey" material — captivating eyes, beautiful in every way, and when she gave you a friendly hug, you felt you were in heaven!

My friends used to tease me and say that I should ask her on a date, but I was too scared. What if she said no — that would break my heart. I would rather have her be my girlfriend in my dreams than have her reject me in reality. My friends, knowing I might never ask her out, gave me an ultimatum. If I didn't ask her out by Friday, they were going to ask her out *for* me. I was in a panic. If I asked her now, she would probably reject me and leave me crushed. But if I left it to my friends, they would embarrass me, and I would become a laughingstock.

I mustered up my courage and called her on the phone. When she picked up, I told her I wanted to take her out to see the latest Will Smith movie this weekend. (I had done my research and knew how much she loved Will Smith. 😊) There was a long silence that felt like an eternity. Voices in my head were screaming, *Why did you have to open your big mouth? You know she would never go with you. Get ready for her to say a big, fat NO!*

Finally, she replied. "OK – see you on Saturday."

I stuttered, "Saturday?"

"Yes. You said this weekend, right? Can we go to my local cinema at Surrey Quays?"

"Of course," I replied in disbelief.

"OK, see you on Saturday," and she hung up.

I sat in disbelief for almost an hour. She had said yes. I'M GOING ON A FIRST DATE!!! I had to pinch myself constantly to make sure I wasn't dreaming.

I called Kay straightaway and said, "Thank you so much – your 'make sure you research' advice has really helped me." I then went on tell him about how I was taking her to see a Will Smith movie. Kay gave me even more valuable advice. "Andrew, make sure you look good and smell nice on your date. No one wants to sit next to someone in a cinema who doesn't smell nice!" So, I made sure I went to a barber, and on the way to the date, I popped into Boots to use some of their tester bottle aftershave (I couldn't afford to buy an actual bottle).

I got there thirty minutes early and waited around. She came thirty minutes late, but I wasn't annoyed. I was simply happy she actually made it down.

The movie was about to start, so we quickly went to the cinema lobby. I looked around and saw other guys looking at Clare and then looking at me in disbelief. I gave them my toughest "She is with me" look. She wanted a large sweet popcorn and large Coke. I only had enough money for one thing, so I asked if we could share. And we proceeded into the dark cinema as the adverts finished and the movie started.

This was the moment I was waiting for! I knew this was the moment I was going to make my move. As we settled into watching the movie, I tried to put my arm around her, and she brushed me off. I tried again ten minutes later, and she brushed it off again. I was thinking *Wow, maybe she doesn't like an arm around her*. I planned my next move — try to see if I could hold her hand. I slowly moved my hand towards her hand, my heart beating louder and louder as I got closer and closer. Suddenly our hands touched, and a jolt of energy went through my body. She must have felt it too but not in the same way. She gave me a 'You better move your hand or else' look. I quickly withdrew my hand and said "Sorry, I was trying to get some popcorn."

I decided then and there to relax. I was moving too fast; I needed to enjoy the movie and maybe try to make a move on Date #2. We didn't talk for the rest of the movie. As we walked out of the cinema, she kind of gave me a 'friend zone' hug and said thanks for taking her to the film. I told her that I'd like to see her again, to which she replied, "Let's see", and then she went home.

Nothing special or exciting had happened, but I thought it was a decent first date that would lead to many more. On the bus ride home, I was daydreaming about how the next date would be ten times better!

Later that evening, a friend of mine called me up and said, "Oh my God, you wouldn't imagine. A girl has just called me up out of the blue and said she wants to come round to my place right now. She said that she was so bored on a date she had that she just had to come and meet me because she knows I'm fun and exciting."

"Wow, you are the man, bro," I exclaimed. "She just called out of the blue?"

"Hey, just out of the blue," he excitedly proclaimed. In my head, I was asking *God why does this never happen to me?*

"What is the name of the girl?"

He then told me something that rocked my world. "Her name is Clare." The same girl I had just been on a date with! You could imagine how I felt. I was the boring one she was talking about and my friend, unbeknown to him, had gotten my girl because he was more interesting than I was.

I told Kay about all that had happened; he went into analysis mode. "At the beginning of the date, what did you talk about?" I tried to remember. "Hmmm. Things like what time is the movie going to start, how expensive the popcorn is, how I needed to get home before 10:30 pm or I will get in trouble with my parents." Kay started to laugh. I said, "What did I do wrong?"

Between fits of laughter Kay replied, "Andrew, to get someone to like you, you gotta be interesting in the first 10 to 30 seconds. If you are not, it is very difficult to get girls to remain interested in you or like you, and they will end up looking for another person — like Clare did."

"But how can you be interesting if you're not an interesting person?"

"You have to find interesting things to talk about. Exciting things that have happened to others or things you have heard about. You need to be interesting or people will ditch you for someone more entertaining."

The same applies to interviews. You have to be interesting, especially in the first ten seconds of answering any question. No one likes someone who is boring. The minute you come into an interview, your number one goal is to fascinate, intrigue, interest the interviewer, not just with your skills but also with you as a person. The interviewer's thinking, "Could I sit next to this person or work with this person for an extended time?" If you are interesting, the answer is going to be yes; then the rest of the interview is just going to be about your having the right skills required for the job.

ACTION POINT — LIST 5 INTERESTING THINGS ABOUT YOURSELF

You need to make sure you have already prepared interesting things to talk about in an interview. You can do this by looking deep into your life for attention-grabbing facts about yourself or hobbies you're interested in so that you can expand on these in an interview.

- List 5 interesting facts about yourself you could tell about on a date to make someone drawn to you.

OH NO – WHAT AM I DOING HERE?!

It wasn't going well at all. Two weeks into my banking internship and I felt like I just didn't fit in. It was an internship in the UK's biggest bank, and it was on their trading floor, where billions of pounds are traded each day. I had to be there at 7 am, which meant leaving my house at 5:30 because I lived on the outskirts of London. The environment was high energy throughout the day, with a lot of shouting and high-pressure moments since a lot of money was at stake.

No one looked like me, no one talked like me and no one had the same interests as I did. Everyone seemed so intelligent and had multiple degrees. They could talk about anything and sound so polished. As a summer intern, you were assigned to a team. The way the floor was set up, it was all open plan; there were probably over 500 people on the floor but your team was small – around 15 people – so it felt like you only knew a small number of people in an ocean of faces. What made matters even worse was that my team wasn't the chattiest with me. After the first day of saying hello, they focused on their jobs and ignored me, which made me feel very isolated and lost.

I felt too scared to open my mouth to join in on conversations because I thought I would expose myself as being a fish out of water! This fear crippled me, and I ended up being withdrawn, glued to my desk and scared to make eye contact. After two weeks, my direct manager pulled me aside as I was leaving for the weekend.

"No one knows you. If you continue like this, you won't be successful at the firm."

"But no one is making the effort with me."

"You need to focus on making an effort with them; get them to notice you."

That weekend, I was terribly depressed. I spoke with my friends and I was like, "Boys, this ain't for me. Maybe I reached too high and this world is not meant for people like me." My friends encouraged me to not give up; they stressed that I was lucky to be in the position I was in, and I ought to find some way to break through. But you know, when you are already defeated in your mind, you feel like you have nothing more to give.

This is sometimes what affects people who have grown up in completely different worlds from the one they are trying to break into. Some people are good at adapting and can just fit in. Others get insecure because they are intimidated by the goal they are trying to achieve. This affects many students from a lower socio-economic background, such as what I came from. We are so much in awe that we get frozen in our tracks and can't perform to the best of our abilities.

I had never been one to give up, but I felt like such a fraud. I was ready to call HR and say this industry is not for me; I QUIT. Luckily, I spoke to a mentor and she gave me a piece of valuable advice. "Just be yourself, Andrew."

"What! Let people find out I'm different?" I came back. "That's not professional."

"Andrew, being professional doesn't mean everyone has to have the same interests. Being professional is servicing your clients and team with high-quality work." She then ended by suggesting, "Try being yourself for a week and see what happens — you have nothing to lose." The next week I went into the office, and each day I focused on getting at least three people to know the real me. I shared how I'm a DJ on the weekends and my favourite author is Walter Mosley; I joked about the fact I'd never eaten sushi before.

And guess what happened. Members of my team started talking to me more and sharing what they were into. People who were into music talked to me about my DJing, I had long debates with people about various authors and I got taken to a sushi restaurant for the first time in my life! Before I knew it, I went from the guy no one wanted to talk to, to the guy they were begging to come back next year for a full-time job.

The same happens in interviews. If you can open up and talk about the interesting things you do, you will attract people to like you, no matter what background they come from.

ACTION POINT – HOW TO MAKE YOUR UNIQUE EXPERIENCES PROFESSIONAL

Many of you reading this are thinking: *ANDREW, STOP IT! My experiences are not professional enough.* Below is a way to make your experiences professional.

1. Write down three of your most unique experiences.
2. Alongside each experience, write three professional skills you learnt from the experience.
3. Now you have a way of discussing a unique experience in your interview and highlighting the professional skills you learnt.
4. End with how you can use each professional skill in the job.

Here's an example:

Experience — Being a belly dancer on a cruise ship

Professional Skills —

- Dedication – It took me three years to master bellying dancing. I did it by watching YouTube tutorials and practicing four hours each day. I will bring the same level of dedication to this job.
- Ability to work in high-pressure situations – As a belly dancer, all eyes are on you and you can't mess up; if you mess up, you will be fired and not hired anywhere else. I will bring to this role that ability to thrive under immense pressure.
- Excellent customer service – As a belly dancer, your number one goal is to please the audience. I will bring to this role that same level of commitment to high levels of customer service.

ANDREW OSAYEMI

WE HAVE NO CAST!!

It was crunch time. We had gotten funded for the full series of my first TV show project, *Meet the Adebanjos*, but we had no cast! And we were planning to film in eight weeks!! We had somehow managed to get a cast together for the pilot but had never before put together an audition for a TV show of this magnitude! I was completely new to the industry, coming straight from banking, and my business partner, Debra, while an experienced TV producer, had never worked on a sitcom before.

This was something completely new to both of us. We asked experienced people for advice and they all said to reach out to agents — they will be able to find you the best actors in the UK.

When we reached out to the top agents, they all laughed at us. They asked questions like "Where is the show going to air? Oh, you haven't found a TV network yet? How much have you raised? Just £100,000 for seven episodes! Do you know that in the UK a BBC sitcom costs £400,000 for just one episode, and you want to make seven of them for £100,000?" They laughed us out the door!!

They said there was no way they were going to send their professional actors to go and audition with a new production company – one that had no track record and had never made anything before – with no TV deal and not enough money to pay their top actors.

So, we were stuck and had to do the next best thing. We just put out adverts on actor freelance websites — the same websites we had used for our pilot. These were websites that let anyone who had a dream to be an actor but wasn't represented by an agent put up their profile; they also allowed companies like ours to put up new casting opportunities.

We put up our ad for our show and added in the description: This is a pilot show that could launch your career all the way to Hollywood." The reaction to the ad was insane! Way more hopefuls applied than we ever expected! We had to book ten days in a casting studio so that we could see all of them. We were excited — this was our chance for finding Hollywood stars!!

The problem with these websites, unfortunately, is that they didn't vet the actors. They were full of people who wanted to be actors, but there was no way to know who had the talent. Imagine a website for people who want to be on *X-Factor*!

After Day 2 we were almost pulling our hair out. We sat through so many wacky auditions. For example, a role would specify an age range of 18 to 20 and the person turning up to audition would be 60. And they would spend the entire audition trying to convince us they could play an 18-year-old. As soon as each person walked out the door, Debra and I would look at each other as if to say, *What the hell was that?* Sometimes they were so bad I would have to hold my mouth to stop myself from bursting out laughing.

It got to a stage almost four weeks before we were scheduled to shoot that we still hadn't cast anyone. Debra said to me, "We need to go back to the agents and get more professional actors."

"But Debra, the agents said they didn't want to work with us because we were unproven."

"Give me their details and, trust me, I will get us some professional actors."

Within a day, Debra called me and said, "Book a casting room for the weekend. I got us some professional actors." I asked, "How did you manage to get them to work with us?" and she replied, "I told them we were casting for a top-secret BBC pilot series."

This audition was like night and day compared to our previous shambolic experience. When a professional actor walks into the room, they walk in with confidence and try to wow you straight away! On the face of it, they may have never acted in any big role. They could be at the same stage as the actor who was just starting out and was on the freelance acting websites we used before. But they didn't act like they were just starting out. They walked in like they had been acting for years, with the mentality that they will blow you away immediately. I think the fact that they had an agent, that someone had co-signed on their talent, gave them that extra confidence.

I remember the actor who would eventually become one of our main actors (the dad in the show). In real life, he is one of the most in-shape people I know. He even has a six-pack at 50! For that particular audition, he walked in as the character he was going to play — a middle-aged dad. He even came with a fake belly and mannerisms of the character he wanted to portray. He walked in with the attitude and swagger that this role was meant for! From the minute he spoke, he interested us! We were blown away. When he left the room, Debra and I looked at each other and high fived.

Another memorable audition was with an actor who became one of our young stars (the young son on the show). He was only 14 but he already had an agent. He started off his audition by singing a popular song. He was so confident. He even had the confidence to jump on a desk and show us his dance moves as well as spin Debra around. At 14!!

You need to display confidence in yourself if you want people to be confident in you. Before your next interview, I want you to pretend like you have an agent. Pretend that a big-time Hollywood agent has signed you to their agency and co-signed to the world that you are going to be the next Hollywood star! Walk into your interviews with the confidence that you have what it takes; that you are going to blow the interviewers away with your personality and skills!

Do this and you will be surprised how much better your next interview will be.

ACTION POINT — HOW TO BE MORE CONFIDENT

It is difficult to build up confidence if you are nervous and haven't had much experience in a certain setting. A lot of people freeze on the big stage because of nerves and from not preparing for the environment. Below are some tips on how to get more confident.

1. Attend industry networking/insight events filled with people in the profession you want to get into. This way you can meet new people and get used to speaking to people in the industry.
2. Read books on inspirational people and research how they discovered their confidence.

3. Perfect your interesting stories. A well-told story can make the listener think the person telling it is greatly confident!
4. Attend comedy improv group lessons. This will take you completely out of your comfort zone but build up your confidence.
5. Research more about the industry and the role so you are more prepared!
6. Practise, practise, practise!

WHY DON'T I TRY ONLINE DATING?

As I was growing up in the 90s, there was no such thing as online dating. We didn't have Tinder, there was no sliding into anyone's DMs, and we didn't even have any social networks! To find a date, you actually had to go out and gather up the courage to meet people face to face. So it was a surprise for me when one day one of my friends called me and said, "Hey, Andrew, guess what? There is this website called BChat you can use that you can chat with girls on a forum and ask them to come on a date."

I was like, "Wow, you mean you can actually meet girls without them seeing you?" This could be the best ever tool for me as I was struggling to meet girls and chat them up in person. Kay said all you had to do was enter a profile about yourself so that people could get in touch. Kay put in his profile, I put in my profile, and all our friends submitted their profiles. We hit submit and we waited to get responses.

Almost immediately, the computer started to go ding, ding, ding, ding, ding, ding, and Kay was getting responses to his profile. When it came to me, I waited, and I waited, and I waited. "This website is rubbish. It doesn't work properly. Do I need to resubmit my profile? Because maybe there was error since we all submitted at the same time," I muttered when I didn't get anything all. But all of my friends got requests.

All of a sudden, the next day, I received a ping. I got a request. Someone wanted to chat with me. I was so excited. For about a month we exchanged messages online. I was falling in love. I felt like this person was my soulmate. Back then we weren't able to send each other pictures of what we looked like, so we had to rely on what we told each other. From the description the girl gave I felt like, *Damn, she is a super model!* We quickly agreed to meet in Charing Cross (a central, busy train station in London). I printed out the profile of my contact, and when I got there I waited; I looked around, and I looked around, and I looked around, and I couldn't find her. We had agreed to meet at 12 o'clock outside the WHSmith store but it was already 1 o'clock and there was no sign of her. I walked around, I looked around, I couldn't find the person.

All of a sudden, I got a tap on the shoulder. She said, "Hi, my name is Jackie from the website." I turned around, but this wasn't the Jackie that was described in the profile. She wasn't the same height. She didn't have the same body composition. She wasn't even the same colour she described in her profile. I was catfished before the original catfish had even been invented, and she was totally not my type. She said "I've been waiting for the past 1 hour. I wasn't sure whether to approach you because I wasn't sure how you would react when you saw me."

As you can imagine, the date didn't go well at all. It was a disaster, and I went back home thinking, *What did I do wrong? Why did only one person decide to get in contact with me when all my friends had over 10 dates from the website. Also, why did I attract someone who completely lied to me?*

Kay said, "Look, let me have a look at your profile." And then he started to laugh. He said, "Andrew, your profile sounds dead, bruv. You have written that you like to read books, like to go for walks. You play the flute. You put down you have never had a girlfriend before. That you are looking to get married as soon as you fall in love. You are only going to attract the desperate girls. People want someone who's a bit more exciting. You have to make yourself sound more interesting on paper so that your profile stands out and people say, "I gotta meet him!"

I said, "Wow, really?" And then I looked at Kay's profile. His profile highlighted the fact that he loved martial arts. He is a r&b singer, a model and excellent dancer. His favourite fashion designers are Versace and Iceberg. It said that although he is has had loads of girlfriends in the past, he is looking for the special one. And he added he is an amazing cook and can't wait to treat you to a candlelight meal! I was like, "Wow, your profile sounds a lot more interesting than mine."

He said, "Yes, that's the trick. If you want people to select you, to meet you or even reach out to you to discuss and find out more about you, you need to be interesting on paper."

ACTION POINT – HOW TO STAND OUT ON PAPER

You need to make sure you are interesting on your CV and application form. You want anyone from HR who looks at your CV to scream, "OMG, I need to meet this person. They sound so interesting." You then need that person to forward your CV on and say to people, "Check this person out."

You can present this on your CV by doing the following:

- Send your current CV to a friend without warning and ask them to tell you what three things stand out to them about your CV.
- Review your friend's feedback and add three more amazing things on your CV that would make someone stay, "Wow!"

- Highlight those three new things with their own heading and bullet points
- Within the bullet points you need to quantify the impact you made and give context, in case someone doesn't know what you are talking about (i.e., Out of 5000 runners in the 800-meter run, I was Number 1 in the region). .
- Make sure all your major sections are highlighted properly and formatting is consistent throughout.
- Get your CV and cover letter checked by friends and family or by careers service at school/university.

MUM, DAD – I'M TAKING A GAP YEAR!

I needed a job desperately. I had just finished my A-Levels and didn't have a university to go to. The previous year my teachers had predicted low grades for me on my university application, which meant I was rejected from all the top schools. I was faced with a choice: apply for the universities that would accept the lower predicted grades or bet on myself, don't apply, and study hard to get higher final grades. What do you think I did? Bet on myself, of course. And it ended up paying off as I was able to achieve much higher grades than my teachers predicted. However, I was still faced with the problem that I didn't have university to go to. Most people in my shoes would have gone through a clearing system. This was a scheme where you call up universities after you got your grades to see if they have any last-minute spaces. However, it was awfully hard to get the best courses through that method since all the good courses were already filled. So, I decided to wait for a year and take a gap year.

You can imagine coming home to Nigerian immigrant parents, who have come to the UK and sacrificed so much for their children, and saying, "Mum and Dad, I don't wanna go to university yet. I wanna take a gap year!!"

"GAP YEAR?" they gasped. "What is that?"

"Mum, Dad — it's when you take a year out to find yourself and develop as a person before going to university," I explained.

"So, you mean you want to not go to uni so you can stay at home and party with your useless friends for one year. No, no, no. Not in our house!!!"

My parents gave me an ultimatum. If I were to stay at home during this gap year, I had to get a full-time job and pay rent. That way they felt I wouldn't waste the year and also wouldn't fall into the trap of hanging out with the wrong crowd of people. So, I needed to get a job fast, or I would be kicked out.

A friend of mine was in the same situation. We were both looking for work during our gap year. She told me that there was a company called Reed, a job recruitment company, which helped people find jobs.

She helped me with my CV, which was really bad. She worked with me on highlighting the skills I had gotten from my experience working at McDonald's, the Crystal palace football stadium, even in sports teams at school. We both applied and got about eight interviews each. I started to think, "This is simple. All I need is to do well in one out of the eight interviews and I will get a job. Easy, right?"

Most of the interviews were done over the telephone, which I thought made it even easier. Before the interviews, they even told us how they were going to interview us. They called it competency-style interviews.

I asked my friend what a competency style interview was, and she told me it's a style of interview where they ask you for any examples that can show you have the skills they are looking for. They could ask you about a time you had to lead a team, for example, and all you have to do is tell them about a time when you led a team.

Is that it? That sounds easy. She said, it might be easy, but you have to make sure you answer in the STAR method. What is the STAR method? It's when you answer their question by first explaining the SITUATION of the example you are talking about, and then you move on to explain the TASK you had to solve; then the ACTION you did, and the end RESULT you were able to achieve. STAR stands for SITUATION, TASK, ACTION, RESULT. My friend said that in a competency-style interview they have a scoring system and judge all your answers on how well you used the STAR method.

So, I made sure I searched online for typical competency interview questions (questions on leadership, dealing with difficult customers, working under pressure, etc.) and made sure I had examples set out in the STAR method.

Over the course of a week, we both had interviews with all the potential employers. When we got the results of the interviews, my friend had 7 out of 8 firms offer her a job. I got 0 out of 8. When I asked for feedback, the only feedback I got was: I didn't connect with the interviewer.

I was pissed. I called my friend. I said I used the formula you told me – this bloody STAR formula – and that didn't work! "OK," she said, "Let me see if you used it right." She asked me what I would say, for example, to a question like: Tell about a time when you had to take a leadership position?

I answered by talking about a time when I took the lead in my school coursework. Before I could finish, she stopped me, laughing. "OMG, you started off super boring. You probably lost the interest of your interviewer. You gotta grip their attention within the first ten seconds and make them want to learn what happened next."

I said, "Wow, you sound like my friend Kay. How would *you* have answered the question?"

She said she would have started off with, "A time I had to take a leadership position was when I was at carnival with my best friend and she collapsed in the middle of thousands of people."

I gasped. "Wow, that sounds way better than what I said. You got me wanting to hear what you did."

"That's why I got as many job offers as I did. You gotta have them hooked in any interview answer you give within ten seconds or you've lost them."

"But isn't that unprofessional — talking about carnival?" I challenged.

"No, you can talk about anything as long as you can demonstrate professional skills. And the more unique and interesting, the better."

I took her advice and aced my very next interview. I ended up working for a year at a company called First National Motor Finance — all because I made a formula interesting. My having a job made my parents happy, and at the end of the one year, I decided I had enough of working and was going to uni. My parents gave me back all the rent I had paid to help pay for my student accommodation.

ACTION POINT — A FRAMEWORK TO ANSWER COMPETENCY QUESTIONS IN AN INTERESTING WAY

Many interviews use competency questions, such as 'Tell me about a time when you did something'. These types of questions require you to use an example from your past to illustrate you have the required skills for the internship. The biggest mistake is people use boring examples that suck the life out of the interviewer. Below is a framework I have developed to make your answers more interesting.

Setting the Scene – How can you make this as interesting as possible? You have 10 seconds to make someone wonder what happened next.
Thought process – What are the different options you were considering to fix the situation?
Actions – What did you do to resolve the situation?
Result – What was the end result?
Learnings – End strong with a moral message about what you learnt.

See how I use the framework to answer this typical interview question:

Tell me about a time you had to solve a complex problem.

Setting the Scene – How can you make this as interesting as possible? Does it make someone wonder what happened next?	On a walk on top of a cliff, a friend slipped and hung onto the edge.
Thought process – What are the different options you were considering to fix the situation.	1) Get help 2) Try help him myself
Actions – What did you do to resolve the situation?	I ran to get a rope, tied it to a tree, and threw it to him.
Result – What was the end result?	A passer-by and I were able to pull him back up.
Learnings – End strong with a moral message about what you learnt.	I learnt never to walk close to the edge of cliffs and the power of teamwork.

What you need to do is focus on having interesting scenes and on having the interviewers on the edge of their seats. Dig for interesting examples from your life and practise on people. Practise your stories on people and get their feedback. Say, "Is this a boring story? Would you want to hear more?" Just practise setting the scenes for your answers and ask people, "Is this interesting enough? Would you like to know how it turned out?" That will give you a sense of whether or not the situations you are describing are interesting enough.

Practise using my framework on typical competency questions with the main focus on making the interviewer think within 10 seconds of you answering: What happened next?

BEING A WINGMAN FOR KAY

It was a cold day in January and Kay called me out of the blue. "Andrew, I need a wingman for a date I'm going on tonight. My date is bringing her best friend along and I need someone to come and keep the friend company while I chill with my date."

I had been a wingman many times and it never ended well. Kay's date was always stunning, and the friend was never anyone's type. It was always a struggle keeping the friend entertained. Kay, sensing my hesitancy said, "Andrew, please. I need your help. Look how much I have been helping you with girls."

I couldn't lie, Kay had been a tremendous help. So, on a cold Saturday Kay and I arrived at Charing Cross train station ready to go on a double date. Kay's date turned up looking like a model straight out of a magazine. Her friend, on the other hand, looked like a boxer who wanted to kill someone in the ring. She always had a permanent scowl on her face.

Kay and his date walked ahead as we strolled through Leicester Square to a place where all the young people hung out. It was a video arcade centre called Trocadero. My date tried to make small talk, but I didn't really have much to say, so our conversations wouldn't go anywhere and just died. To be honest, I was a bit rude and not engaging much in conversation. Up in front, I could see Kay and his date laughing and having what looked like an amazing time.

All of a sudden, a big group of girls bumped into Kay and his date in front of us. One of the group, a girl even more stunning than Kay's date, whispered something and, all of a sudden, they all looked and stared at me. Kay quickly headed over.

"Andrew, you are not going to believe it, but that girl over there just told my date she thinks you are nice. I think you should talk to her." I thought, *OMG, I am being pranked*. But then I thought, *This is my reward for being a faithful wingman.*

As I prepared myself to walk over, the vibe suddenly changed. Kay's date called him back over. "Forget it, she said she changed her mind."

"What, in ten seconds? What happened?" Kay asked.

Kay's date explained, "My friend told her that Andrew was boring, rude, and doesn't make an effort at all. That she shouldn't even bother with you." All because I was rubbish at small talk with someone unrelated, it had messed up my chances with this supermodel.

The same happens in interviews. You never know when you are being judged. From the minute you enter the building of an interview, you need to be ON. From being nice to the doorman and receptionist, engaging in friendly small talk in the lift, on the walk to the interview room, or just before an interview is starting — you never know when you are being judged!

ACTION POINT – WORK ON YOUR SMALL TALK

Task: Watch TED talks and read books on how to master small talk. Make sure you read the popular news websites before your interview and be able to talk to anyone about the top trending things happening in the world on the day of your interview. Also, be able to talk about the weather, transport, etc.

COMMON INTERVIEW QUESTIONS THAT YOU NEED TO MAKE INTERESTING

Use all you have learnt during this chapter to make the answers to the following questions more interesting:

- Tell me about a time when you had to deal with a difficult team member.
- Tell me about a time you had to solve a complex problem.
- Tell me about a time when you failed at something.
- Sometimes we have to make decisions that are challenged by others. Describe a situation when you made a decision that was challenged.
- What is the biggest risk you have ever taken in your life?
- Tell me about a time when you found it difficult to keep someone's attention.
- What is your greatest weakness?
- Which books do you like reading?

CHAPTER THREE

YOU GOTTA BACK IT UP!

DANCING AT THE HOUSE PARTY

I was at a house party with Kay. The music was pumping, the lights were low, and everyone was having a great time. I watched a girl who caught my eye, and after an hour I finally got up the courage to ask her if she wanted to dance. Silently, she nodded, and we started dancing to a song by dancehall artist Bennie Man. However, we were slightly out of step. When she went left, I went right; when she went right, I went left. Our legs started to bash, and within thirty seconds she stopped, shook her head and walked away to hang out with her friends.

For the rest of the night, when I went to ask other girls to dance, they all said NO. I went back to Kay, who was having the time of his life, and asked him what I was doing wrong. He said, "Andrew if you ask someone to dance, you also have to back it up with good dancing. In life, people will give you a chance at the beginning but will quickly dismiss you if you can't back up your words with action."

He went on to say that word gets around fast if you are all talk and no action. "Andrew, all the girls who turned you down to dance probably saw you dancing badly or heard you can't dance!!! No one wants to dance with someone that has that bad a reputation."

The next day, I started to master all the popular dance moves of the day. I was determined that next time I asked a girl to dance I would be able to back it up with great dancing!!

The same applies to interviews. People are willing to give you a chance, but you have to back up everything you say you can do with evidence. The interviewer is like that girl at the party:

[70]

they want to know if you are all talk or actually have what it takes. The way you do that in an interview is to back up what you're saying with examples.

ACTION POINT — CREATE EXAMPLES ALONGSIDE YOUR SKILLS

I want you right now to think about five things that make you the best person for a role (i.e., you're hard-working, an excellent communicator, an exceptional salesperson, you can work under pressure, you're good with data, you have an eye for detail, etc.). Your list should focus on your skills and what makes you stand out as qualified for the role.

Now, under each point I want you to try to write three examples that back up each point you say you are good at. If you are struggling on any point, maybe you need to dig deeper into your experiences or find another point to highlight.

I'M A HUSTLER, BABY!

When I was growing up, I always wanted to be an entrepreneur. Being raised by working-class, immigrant parents who had just enough money for the family in terms of food, schooling and everything else, we were always taught that if you want money, you have to go make it for yourself.

So, from a super-young age, I was always working. One of my first jobs, when I was around 12 years old, was handing out flyers for a fast food restaurant near my house. You got paid by how many flyers you distributed, so I would be out handing out flyers from early in the morning to late in the evening. I advanced to working at McDonald's at the age of 16. I remember at the interview they said the only position they had was an early morning shift at five o'clock. That was the time I sometimes got in from parties, but I desperately needed money to buy clothes to look good for the parties, so I had to take the job and sometimes have only a couple of hours of sleep between partying and leaving for work.

I even hustled my way into working as a steward for the local football team, called Crystal Palace, at 17. They were only allowed to employ people from 18 upwards, and they kept asking me for my tax ID documentation (National Insurance). I kept saying I was waiting for my National Insurance card to arrive, which would confirm my age, but because I kept turning up when they were understaffed on match day, they kept employing me and asking me to bring in my documentation next time!

At school, it was the same. I was always hustling and making money. At 11 I got a scholarship to go to a private school through a scheme that paid the school fees for students from deprived neighbourhoods. I grew up in social housing in a deprived part of London, and I went to one of the worst primary schools in the country. So, I was lucky — out of the hundreds of thousands of students who applied, I was able to get the full paid scholarship. Everything was paid for – my travel to school, my school uniform, school dinners — everything!

At first, it felt very embarrassing for me to go there. The school was in a completely different neighbourhood than where I lived, I had to take three buses to get to the school (which took over an hour) and I got teased back home because the school uniform was so different from everyone else's.

But the experience in the school completely opened my eyes and introduced me to a new world of people who lived completely different from how I lived. Very quickly, I found out how to make money. I found out that many of the rich kids in the school loved R&B and hip-hop music but didn't know where to buy the albums, as their parents banned them from listening to it. So, I ran a business — getting albums from people who were selling them on the street in my local area and selling them to the rich school kids. This made me enough money to buy things for Christmas, and so on and so forth. I have always been and always will be an entrepreneur. At the age of 18, I decided to take things up to a whole completely new level.

My cousin John and I were big partygoers. We used to go to a lot of clubs. In fact, at one stage we went clubbing at least five times a week. Because we were always in the clubs, we started to get friendly with the club promoters, who shared with us how much money they were making from the ticket sales of people coming each night. Club promoters were always the flashiest, had the best cars, and always had the most beautiful women chasing after them because they controlled who got into the hottest clubs!

One night on the drive back from a club, we had a light bulb moment. Why don't we start our own club business? We could begin by inviting all our friends, their friends, and other regular club-goers to our club nights. We would make so much money. Also, I was secretly thinking this would make me a hit with the ladies! So, we decided to try to become club promoters.

However, when we went around speaking with different clubs to find a venue, no one wanted to give us their club for us to host our club nights. "You have no track record," is what we were constantly told by club managers. I remember walking into meetings with club owners and managers. We would come in dressed looking slick, trying to pretend like we were big-time club promoters with loads of confidence. But, when they asked us questions like, What club nights have you done before? How many people could you guarantee will attend?, we would say things like, "We can guarantee we could bring in at least over 500 people." They would look at us and start laughing.

"We've seen people like you before. You come in, you say you can guarantee 500, and only 5 people show up. We're going to have to charge you over a thousand pounds for you to rent our club."

"A thousand pounds? Are you having a laugh? We heard you give clubs to people for free," John would reply.

They said, "Yes, we do. But those are for people who have a track record. You have no track record, so the cost of hiring our club is £1,000."

We would storm out of the meeting, super pissed off. But if you look at it from the club owners' perspective, they had to charge us because they made their money from drinks. And if they opened and only five people came out, and they gave us the club for free, they would lose money. So, to offset that, they decided to charge us a minimum amount that would cover their costs.

Sometimes in life, you have to look at your situation and say *Screw this, we are going to prove ourselves no matter what.* Even if people don't believe in you, you have to make them believe. So, John and I decided, "Look, if it cost £1,000, let's get the money together and pay for the use of the club."

We created a promotional unit called the Cautious Family, which was me, John, Debra (who would go on to become my TV production partner), and John's younger brother, Peter. And we all put money together, £250 each, into renting a club in New Cross for £1000. We then went everywhere in London for a month with our flyers, promoting all over the city for our first club night.

Very quickly, the night of the event rolled around. The doors opened at 10 o'clock and we stood at the front of the club, dressed like Miami beach club promoters; looking slick with our white shoes, white trousers and flowery shirts. But when we opened the doors there was no one there. No queue. At 10:30 pm only ten people had arrived even though we had promoted the club night as being free before 10:30 pm in order to get an early crowd into the event. At 11 pm, there were only twenty people in the club, and we started to sweat. John and I looked at each other, thinking *Wow, we have blown it*. The club manager was eyeing us like, "Look at these jokers. They thought they could be club promotors. Good thing we charged them £1000." To get away from all the shameful glances, I snuck away to a late-night chicken and chips restaurant. I just wanted to get away because I was feeling the stress.

Around 12 o'clock, as I walked back to the club from barely eating my meal, I saw a queue. Not just any queue; a queue of over 100 people. At one o'clock, when I came back out to check, there was still a queue of 100 people. By the end of the night, over 750 people had attended that club night. Over 750 people; 250 more than we guaranteed. And we made a killing. We made a killing all because we were ready to back ourselves.

Sometimes in life, if you don't have the track record you have to go out there and create a reputation so that people take you seriously. And because we backed it up, after that day we got many offers from many different clubs across London, giving us their venue for free.

ACTION POINT — HOW TO BUILD CREDIBILITY

Do you lack credibility at the moment? Are you claiming you can do all the things required for the internship, but you lack the credibility or evidence? Then you need to take it into your own hands to start building credibility. What societies, groups, voluntary work or part-time work can you do to boost your credibility? Sometimes it involves giving your skills or work away for free just to build a track record. It could involve starting an entrepreneurial venture just to prove you have the skills. Whatever it is you want, you need to build some credibility.

Write down three things you can do to build more credibility for the internship you want to do. Spend the next 90 days doing it.

RAISING £100,000 WITH NO TRACK RECORD

There was a time when I was asking for money from investors for my TV production company before we had even created anything. I needed to raise over £100,000. I used to go around from pillar to post, asking people I knew from working in banking, "Can you invest £10,000? £5,000? £1000? £500?"

Everyone said no. They were like, "Andrew, you used to work in a bank; what do you know about TV? We have not seen anything you've made. Do you even know how to use a video camera? How do we know whether or not people will like it?" If I were in their shoes, I would have been thinking the same thing. I was asking for money for something I had never done and had no evidence to back up whether I knew what I was doing.

My cousin Debra was a TV producer. She said, "Look, Andrew, let's make a pilot so we can show people our vision."

"How much will it cost?"

"About 5 thousand."

So, we both decided to put money in to make the pilot. I had some money from my banking days, so it was easy for me to invest, but Debra didn't have any money at all. Yet she believed so much in the project, she sold her cherished car to raise her share. You can imagine how she felt — risking it all for this project with someone who had no history of creating anything in his life.

Once we made that pilot, we then put it on YouTube. I still remember the feeling of constantly refreshing the page in the hope of seeing if our video's views had gone up. After an hour we only 40 views; after six hours, only 150 views. The gamble hadn't paid off. I called Debra and she also sounded depressed. "Well, at least we tried," I consoled. "Let's see how it does tomorrow," she sighed.

The next day we had only 200 views.

Debra tried to call me, but I didn't pick up. You know that feeling when you know something has been a flop and you don't want to talk about it? That was what I was feeling. After her fifth attempt, I turned off my phone and went back to my room to sleep.

The next day I thought, *Let me just check and see how many views we have*. I went and hit the refresh button on the computer. It was on 5,000 views. Wow. I called Debra. "Debra, are you seeing this? Are you seeing this? We have 5,000 views!" She was like, "Yes, that's what I was trying to call you about." She told me after getting off the phone with me the previous night she had spent the whole night emailing our trailer to bloggers and news websites, telling them about our story of two independent producers trying to get a sitcom made against the odds. She had also gotten flyers and posters printed and put up across London.

By the end of that week, we had 25,000 views. We were elated. In a few weeks, we had over 75,000 views. Within a month, because we had backed up our vision with actual numbers of people around the world watching our pilot, and loads of comments about how they wanted to see it made into a series, all the investors were convinced in our vision and we were able to raise over £100,000.

If you can back up your claims with quantifiable evidence, you will be surprised how quickly someone will believe in you and decide to take a chance on you with your dream internship.

ACTION POINT – QUANTIFIABLE EVIDENCE

A key reason why people fail at interviews is because all they use is buzzwords and nothing else. They say I'm hard working. I have a commitment to excellence. I'm dedicated. I have a willingness to learn. I'm determined. I'm good with numbers. I'm analytical. I have strong attention to detail. Blah, blah, blah, blah, but you never provide any examples/evidence of these skills.

What people are looking for is quantifiable evidence – actual numbers/data to back up your claims. Using quantifiable evidence will make any claims you provide so much stronger. People like numbers. For example, you're applying for a sales internship and you're asked, "Why do you think you'll be a good person to hire for this sales internship?" If you say, "It's because I'm hard working, I'm a good communicator and a people person", and that's all you say, you probably won't get the internship.

But if you say, "Because in every sales role I've done, I've always been the top performer. While working at Car Phone Warehouse, I increased sales by 50% and generated an average 5,000 sales a day, which was 2,000 more than anyone else in the store," you'll most likely be asked when you want to start.

- For your three key examples of why you should be hired, can you write impressive quantifiable evidence? If not, then you need to get some impressive numbers, so you stand out!

HIGH STAKES POKER

Sometimes, lying about your accomplishments can get you into a lot of trouble. Two years after joining my full time banking job, I was living in New York. I had been sent by the bank to be the head Euro/USD trader in our New York office. The package I'd been given to go there was fit for a king! I was living in a one-bedroom penthouse flat in the middle of Manhattan, 1000 square feet on the 38th floor overlooking the East River — and it was all being paid for by the bank. My living room was so big that I was able to have a full-sized pool table, sofas and dining table, and there was still enough space to throw parties with over 100 people. Not bad for the guy who grew up in Peckham with nothing but dreams!

I lived by myself. My family and friends were thousands of miles away, and during the weekend I got bored and lonely. Having no close friends and being bored with a lot of money to spend adds up to a bad combination. I remember bumping into someone at a bar who said, "Andrew, tell me what you're interested in," and I said, "Oh, when I was at university, I used to love deejaying, partying and playing poker." My mention of poker pricked his ears up, and he was like, "Wow, I'm interested in poker too. There are some underground poker games that I could invite you to."

You see, betting on poker in New York at that time wasn't 100% legal, so there were underground poker games that enthusiasts could go to. You could play poker without having to travel hundreds of miles away to the Atlantic City casinos where it was legal.

But then he tipped me off by saying, "Andrew, I need to warn you: these are big games, where the minimum buy-in is $1000, and thousands can be lost or made in a night. Are you sure you can play in a big game? I don't want you to lose money."

You see, in university I'd played poker; I'd even made lots of money playing poker. But never in games as big as $1000! I played in small tournaments — tournaments where you'd put up £20 to £50 maximum to win thousands and thousands. This was different. This was a cash game where you'd have to put down your actual money and you could lose unlimited amounts of money in one game.

However, my ego took over and I replied "Of course. Don't worry. I'm used to playing in big games. It's OK, a $1000 buy-in is nothing to me." So, he brought me into some of the games. When I first started out, I did fantastic. I mean, I would buy in for $1000 and at the end of the night have made $3000–$5000. It was incredible. However, because I started winning, I got introduced to bigger games and bigger games, where the minimum buy-in was even higher!

Needless to say, very quickly I started to lose and not just lose small amounts – I was losing big!!! This was because these larger games were played completely different from the games I had played before, and I was in way over my head.

One crazy incident happened in one of the games that finally convinced me to stop. I was playing well and this time I was actually winning!! Suddenly, three masked men burst through the door waving guns and told everyone to get on the ground. They pointed a gun to everyone's heads and told them to empty all their money, jewellery and phones into a bag. They robbed the place dry! As I lay on the floor with a gun pointed to my head, all I could think was *Look what lying gets you, Andrew. You could have just been honest from the start and you wouldn't have been here.* I vowed then to make sure that I would live a life of being honest about my accomplishments. If I ever found myself lacking skills, I would do a course or upskill myself instead of lying and ending up over my head. I have taken this mindset forward ever since and I'm happy to say I have avoided guns being pointed at me.

Don't lie about your accomplishments, as this can come back to bite you in the future as it did for me in poker.

ACTION POINT- HONESTY CHECK

Look through your CV and make sure you haven't got anything on there that is untrue. You don't want to be caught out during an interview or, even worse, when you have the job.

If you feel your CV or experience is lacking, now is the time to do volunteering work, free work or part-time work to enhance it. Also, don't be afraid to use examples in your interview from non-work experiences like volunteering, hobbies and sports. You would be surprised how what would seem to be unrelated experience could convince someone you are good for a job. I remember a student who used as an example of his skills his being a carer for his poor parents. All the skills that the job required included the same hard work, diligence, attention to detail he was able to demonstrate, having already experienced them through being a carer.

COMMON INTERVIEW QUESTIONS THAT YOU NEED TO BACK UP YOUR ANSWERS

Use all you have learnt during this chapter to back up your answers to the following questions.

- You say you are good at sales. Can you expand on that and give me some examples?
- Tell me about a time you led a team to achieve great success.
- Tell me about a time you changed the culture in a team.
- You say you succeed despite the odds; give me an example.
- You mentioned you are hardworking; can you expand on that and give me some examples?
- Give me an example of when you used your entrepreneurial skills to create new revenue in a company.

CHAPTER FOUR

YOU NEED TO HAVE A 'WHY YOU' STORY

SHE SMILED BACK AT ME!

It was a hot summer Saturday and Kay and I were hanging out the Whitgift Centre, a shopping centre in South East London. We weren't there to buy anything — we were BROKE! We were there to hang out with friends and see if we could bump into any new girls we could talk to.

As Kay and I made the loop around the shopping centre for what seemed the one-millionth time, I saw a girl out of the corner of my eye who simply just blew my breath away. I couldn't help myself; I ended up just staring at her like a deer caught in headlights. She spotted me staring and, to my surprise, she smiled back. Not just any smile – it was a warm, inviting smile. A smile that said, "I want to get to know you because I think you are cute." Kay, who had just noticed her, said, "Damn, who is that? She is fine. Andrew. OMG, she is smiling at you. You gotta go and talk to her."

Kay pushed me forward and, with the girl watching, I reluctantly and slowly strolled over to her. In my head, all I could think was *What am I going to say?* When I finally got up to her, I seductively smiled and said, "Can I have your number?" She looked at me funny and came back with, "Tell me why I should give it to you."

That kind of threw me off because I was either expecting a no or a yes. I didn't expect to have to defend why I was asking, so I started to stutter, "Urrrrr ummmmm." No words were coming out. I started to sweat. A few awkward seconds passed and finally, after a minute, the girl's friend pulled her away and the girl gave me one last look, almost sad that I had not taken my opportunity to get her number. And just like that — she was gone. I went back to Kay and explained what happened. He shook his head and said, "Bro, you always need to be ready with your sales pitch of WHY YOU. Always be prepared to sell yourself!"

In any interview you attend, whether it's a formal or informal setting, you will be asked at one point in the interview: *Why do you want this internship? Why should we hire you?* That's when you need to have your 'why you' story prepared, your sales pitch ready. Why you? This is where you must sell WHY YOU.

ACTION POINT — 100 WORD 'WHY YOU'

- Write down a 100-word answer on why you should be hired. Now, is it unique? Does it inspire any emotion? Do you back it up with evidence?

This section will give you tips on how you can improve this exercise.

INVITED TO SPEAK AT HARVARD

After finally overseeing the successful launch of Season 1 of my TV show, *Meet the Adebanjos,* I was expecting it would be easier for me to get Season 2 off the ground. I thought there would a queue of TV stations lining up, offering truckloads of money for a second season.

In fact, getting Season 2 created was impossible. No TV station wanted to pay the amount of money it would cost to make Season 2. For eighteen months after the first season was released, I travelled all over the world trying to make a deal. Every time, I would come so close before the deal collapsed at the last moment. I had so many promises broken, and I'm honest enough to say that it broke me. I was emotionally and physically exhausted. I had given my all on this venture – sacrificed a career in investment banking – and it was all for nothing. You could imagine how I felt in my tiny bedroom in my parents' house, which I had to move back into because I was flat broke!!!

Then, out of the blue, I got an email from Harvard University say they were inviting me to the Africa Business Conference to come and speak about TV in Africa.

My initial reaction was, *HELL NO, forget that.* This was because, on the face of it, this looked like another set-up for failure; another conference where I would go and speak, everyone would clap, and nothing would come from it. And, trust me, I had done plenty of those speeches at conferences over the eighteen months of trying to get the show off the ground. And what added insult to injury was, they were not even going to pay for travel all the way to Boston from the UK. They said they didn't have a budget to fly any of the speakers over, but this would be great exposure for me! Exposure is what I had been promised by so many conferences that I had ended up spending a fortune going to, only to have it never lead to anything. The crazy thing was, I didn't even have a way to get there if I wanted to. I was so broke. It was two years since I had left banking and I had rinsed out my savings and was maxing out my credit cards. I didn't even have enough money to put petrol in my car, so how was I going to find money to pay for a flight and accommodations in Boston?

I also felt like I was a fraud. A fake. Someone who walked around and said everything is going well, keeping up the image that I was making big moves but deep down I had nothing going on!

I mentioned the Harvard conference to my good friend Emeka, who was also one of the investors in my company. He was ecstatic that I was getting that type of opportunity to speak at a conference of that calibre, and he couldn't understand why I was so against going. "Look, Andrew, you need to get your head up, you need to stay positive. You need to go."

"But Emeka, I'm not feeling it," I said, "I just can't put myself in that environment and have to pretend to everyone."

He said, "You need to go. You never know what might happen."

"But I don't have the money, Emeka."

"I'll pay for your ticket."

"But I can't face going all by myself."

"I'll come with you."

So, we ended up on a plane going to Boston, and all the way there, Emeka was by my side, giving me words of encouragement and hyping me up! Once we got to the event, we found out there had been a change of line-up on my panel. Sitting alongside me on the panel was the head of the biggest TV station in Africa — the same person I had been trying to get a meeting with for months! Someone I'd been emailing and trying to contact to help me get Season 2 off the ground, to no avail! And right now, she and I were going to be equals on a panel together, in front of hundreds of people. Emeka said, "This could be the chance you have been waiting for, Andrew! Make sure you have your sales pitch ready!"

During the panel, when it was my time to speak, I was like a Pentecostal preacher! Passionately speaking about the show and whipping the audience up into a frenzy about our plans for a new season, I got a standing ovation. The TV head looked around in awe at the response of the crowd and whispered to me. "Let's meet for lunch after this panel."

At lunch, the first thing she said to me was, "Why should we buy your TV show?" I dove straight into my sales pitch. "Look, you need to buy this TV show. One, because there's nothing like it in your market. It allows Africans in Africa to see how Africans abroad are acting and behaving. Two, it's fresh, it's funny, it's vibrant. And three, I can give it to you for a great price. Lastly, just know that if you have faith in us, we will deliver for you an amazing show; an amazing product that will elevate your TV station and allow you to win awards."

She looked at me, smiled, and gave me the deal on the spot. She gave me the deal on the spot!! After eighteen months of struggle, I was able to get a deal in thirty minutes. All because

I had my sales pitch prepared to tell the audience on the panel and could tell it to her directly.

I had my 'why the show' story. Do you have a 'why you' story for when you have to sell yourself at an interview, an event, in the lift? You never know who you might meet, so always be prepared and ready to 'sell yourself'.

ACTION POINT — WORK ON YOUR PUBLIC SPEAKING

How good is your public speaking and storytelling? Your ability to communicate and tell a story will have a massive impact on the jobs you get and how far you will rise in that job. You can be called to speak anywhere — in an interview but also on a panel or in front of potential investors. If you can speak convincingly with a powerful 'why you' story, you will impress your potential employers.

Here are some tips to get you better at storytelling —

- Watch the TED talk "The magical science of storytelling" by David JP Phillips on YouTube.
- Buy books on storytelling.
- Practise creating 30- to 60-second stories about your 'why' (i.e., the reason you should hire me is because of my time working as a dishwasher in a restaurant at 10 years old).
- Practise telling your stories with your friends and family and in mock interviews.
- Take their feedback and make your stories better. A good story has been through at least ten drafts before it's polished enough to win the heart and mind of your interviewer.

PS: Make sure you have a friend like Emeka in your life to pick you up when you are down!

I LOVE CHEESY CHAT UP LINES

It was a chilly spring night and Kay and I were rushing out at 2.30am to get to a nightclub. We weren't hoping to get in—it was too late for that. We were rushing to get there as girls started to leave, so we could chat them up. We would dress up like we had been at the club itself or were coming from another club, when in fact we were so broke we couldn't afford to pay to get into clubs until pay day. After driving my mum's busted Vauxhall Astra car round the block ten times, I found a parking spot and quickly Kay and I rushed to the outside of the club so we could be in prime position when girls started to leave at 3am.

Very soon, a sea of beautiful girls started to appear, and Kay and I looked at each other, grinning. We were in heaven. Very quickly we started approaching girls, getting ready to introduce ourselves and hopefully score some telephone numbers to call during the days ahead.

I approached my first potential girlfriend, who smiled warmly when she saw me coming. I started our conversation by saying "Your eyes are like the ocean; I could swim in them all day". Her smile turned into a frown. "That's original", she said sarcastically. I talked for a few more minutes but I could tell her mind wasn't there with me. She quickly rejected my inquires for her number and moved on.

Maybe she had a bad time in the club, I thought. I approached another potential girlfriend and said, "Are you a parking ticket? Because you've got fine written all over you". This girl just shock her head and continued walking on. *Is it my breath?* I thought.

When I approached the third girl, I made sure I was chewing a fresh piece of chewing gum and I said, "If being sexy was a crime, you'd be guilty as charged". She asked me, "How many girls have you said that to? You couldn't think of anything else? I haven't got time for guys who just recycle the same lines all the time."

On the way home, I asked advice from Kay who, as usual, had left with more numbers than he knew what to do with. He said "Andrew, every girl wants to feel special. They can't feel like that if you use lines you got from a chat up book that everyone uses and that you use on everyone else. You have to hook them with something different and interesting that catches their attention." I asked, "What do you say?" He told me, "I always start with a gripping story or something unique to them. Like, remember that girl I got the number from who looked like Beyoncé?" I nodded. "Well, I told her I liked the way she accessorised her shoes with her belt, and then went on to tell her a story about the types of belts rich millionaire women bought when I worked in Selfridges. I had her so hooked that she asked me for my number."

I was gobsmacked. It made so much sense that I ditched the chessy chat up lines. I became more personal and used memorable stories to sell why someone should give me their number which lead to me getting more numbers!!

The same is the case in many interviews. After working in banking for many years, I had a passion to give back—a passion to help students get top internships and full time jobs. So I started to coaching them on interviews and I started hearing the unoriginal answers over and over again.

When I was giving a mock interview and I would ask, "Why should we hire you?" They would answer, "You should hire me for three main reasons: I'm a hard worker, I am someone who thinks outside the box, and I'm someone who has attention to detail. " Or they would say, "You should hire me because I am a quick learner. I'm someone who works very hard and someone who is always on time. "

And, for some reason, no matter what they said afterwards they'd lost me. They were not saying anything original; every student used the same buzzwords. I would start to tune them out and my mind would drift on to other things—just like those women were with me when they heard my cheesy lines.

I started to think, *How can the students make it better? How could they stand out?* I remembered the advice from Kay, who said to start with an original story that grips someone's attention and when imbedded in your story demonstrates all the reasons you should be considered.

So, one day when a student came in and gave me the same standard answer that everyone gave, I stopped him and suggested he start with an interesting story first. One that grips people but isn't generic. A story that would make me think, *I gotta hire you*. He said, "Any story?" and I said yes.

He sat quietly for a minute and then said, "The reason you should hire me is because of my experiences I had escaping the war in Afghanistan." I thought *Wow*. I was hooked. I was ready to listen. He had me. He proceeded to talk about how he came over from Afghanistan when he was young, going through over ten countries before finally getting to the UK. He told me how he made a better life for himself and got into top universities. And that resilience is why someone should hire him.

I thought, *Wow. That is it*. Start with an interesting story first. That grips people and gets them to think they ought to hire this person. And then I started to coach more and more students about starting with a story. One of the interesting things I've heard over the years was a student telling me the reason I should hire him is because of his experience working in a nightclub from the age of ten. Or the applicant who said I should hire him for his experience of how he got over breaking his leg just when on the verge of signing a youth professional football contract. Or the one who said I should hire her because she started a business with £10 that now pays house rent for her parents. Or the applicant who felt I should hire her for how she got over her experience as a failed pop singer.

ACTION POINT – HOW TO BE ORGINAL

Starting with stories grabs people's attention and makes them remember you. Starting with something generic is almost like starting with my generic chat up lines—it turns people off. Focus on starting with a captivating story of something that you've done in your life and use that to demonstrate the skills that illustrate why you should be hired. The story should be the type that, if I held you at gunpoint and told you to tell me two stories, those stories would convince me you have amazing potential.

An Example Structure for Answering "Why You?" with a Story

1. Start your answer with the headings of two captivating stories that showcase your excellence without any further explanation. For example, you might say "You should hire me for my experience running a nightclub at 17" or ".. for my exploits almost qualifying for the Olympics". You want to keep it short and sweet so that

you immediately grab the interviewer's interest and make him want to know more.

2. Expand on both stories to give the interviewer more insight. Make sure your story demonstrates the main skills you want to highlight for the job or internship.

3. End with a strong conclusion that repeats the gist of the two capti

THE GRADUATE HUNGER GAMES

Have you ever watched a *Hunger Games* movie? The film is about twelve young people from different districts in a fictional country. They have been chosen to fight to the death until there is one winner! That movie describes my first graduate job. You see, after university I was so happy that I got that big job — the big job I was desperately looking for, to work in the financial markets as a trader at the Royal Bank of Scotland in their Investment Banking division. But what I wasn't told when I got the graduate job was that it actually wasn't a full-time position. It was just a one-year probational contract where you had to compete with the other new graduates on the programme to find a team that was willing to take you on full time. We were mis-sold the graduate programme. We believed we were going into a full-time job, but instead it was a one-year *Hunger Games* situation where the graduates would have to fight amongst each other to impress a team that would take them on.

As you can imagine, the psychological impact of finding out it was a straight-up fight, after thinking you had a full-time job, was tough on many of the graduates. Many of us went from being friends to being adversaries. The prize was a full-time contract with a large starting salary, which many of us needed desperately, so the competition was fierce! The HR team designed a process that was meant to help teams find the graduates they wanted to hire full time. We were given three rotations in three different divisions of the bank over the one-year period, during which a team could assess our skills. If they liked you, they would hire you. As soon as the first rotation began, the other graduates started backstabbing each other. Some would go around spreading rumours about other graduates to try and convince the team to pass up a graduate.

Some graduates would give you the wrong guidance when you asked for help on a project. That way, you would submit inferior work to your team and, hence, lower your chances of getting hired. It was dog-eat-dog!!

I remember my first rotation. I went there with the right attitude. I worked hard and I made sure I met all my deadlines. But at the end of the rotation, the boss of the team asked me, "Why should we hire you?" I did not really have a strong answer. I replied, "Because I really want to work here, and I think my work speaks for itself." I could see the boss wanted me to say more to convince him, but I left it at that. At the end of the interview, he said, "Thanks for your time on the team. We are still considering our options". I knew what he was actually saying: "You haven't done enough to convince me to hire you."

When I left the meeting, I was kicking myself. *Why didn't I properly sell myself?!* It was because I hadn't really prepared to answer a question that direct. I thought I already had done enough, through my strong work ethic and high-quality work, that I wouldn't have to try that hard to convince them to hire me. But no, he still wanted to know, "Why me"? He wanted me to sell myself. And I struggled to sell myself.

My second rotation was a disaster. The team did not like me; I didn't like the team. It didn't work out. Towards the end of the rotation, they made it very clear that they were not going to hire me.

So, I was down to my final rotation. I remember getting advice from a mentor who said to me, "You need to work on how to sell yourself, Andrew. You work hard. You're good at your job. But you struggle with selling yourself, and people who are not as good as you are getting hired because they are better salespeople."

I started to research how I could sell myself better. First, I started reading many books on salesmanship and how to be confident and persuasive. Every time in life I have found myself lacking in skills or struggling, I have always found a resource to help me improve. Whether it's books, YouTube videos, podcasts, online courses, one to one tuition, etc. I always dive straight into acquiring knowledge so I can get better. But before I could even put all I had learnt to good use, on the first day of my final rotation the boss sat me down and admitted, "Look, Andrew. Before you start, I want to be honest with you because I don't want to waste your time. We have already offered someone else your job."

I was devastated. I remember thinking to myself, *What do I do now? It's all over. My dream of getting a high-paid banking job is over. I've let everyone down!*

One of the key things I learnt from my research on how to sell yourself is that you need to display confidence. Self-confidence allows people to be confident in you. So, I went back to that first rotation, in which I felt I performed well but I wasn't able to sell myself. I went back to the same boss and I said, "Look, I know I am the best person for the role. I want to work in this division. Please give me one more chance."

He was surprised by my confidence but said, "We are already considering another graduate." I countered, "Have you offered the graduate the job yet?" He said, "No" so I countered, "Then give me six more weeks and I guarantee that I will prove to you I am the person you need to hire."

He found a small team and said I could work with them. Immediately, I started to add value, working hard on anything they asked me to do, and I could see they were impressed. But they kept repeating there weren't any graduate roles available.

One day I overheard one of the guys on the team saying he was going to play in a poker game. He was worried he would lose as the players were more experienced than him. I took him aside and I said, "Boss, you know I used to play poker. Here are some tips." And I sat down and taught him some tips I learned from playing poker at university. Over the weekend, he called me many times asking for advice on some of the things that were happening in the game he was playing. Each time, I took his call, I replied to his texts, and I tried to give as much value as possible. In the end, he won a lot of money in that poker game.

On my last day with the team, we went away to conduct the final interview and he started by asking me the all-important question: "Why should we hire you?" This time I was ready. I told him how I could be a full-time asset to the team, gave evidence of all the extra work I had done, and how I had saved the team money through some of the automation I had put in place. And lastly, I added that I could help everyone on their team with their poker games. And that is how I got a full-time position on that team.

You need to be able to demonstrate your 'Why You' by being able to sell yourself and adding value in ways others can't.

ACTION POINT — WHAT DO YOU HAVE THAT CAN ADD VALUE TO A TEAM?

What unique skills and experience do you have that could add value to your potential work colleagues?

- List 3 work skills you have that you can use to add value to the team. Do you have examples? How can you make your skills unique?
- Also, list 3 hobbies you are an expert in (i.e., baking, singing, chess). Find a way to see if anyone on the team has the same interests and use that to build a strong connection with them.

Pro Tip – If given the name of your interviewer, look them up on LinkedIn. Research some of their interests; if there is common ground, ask them questions about it during the interview and try to help with any issues they might have, based on your experiences.

ANDREW OSAYEMI

NETWORKING AT PARTIES

Sometimes you can demonstrate your 'Why You' in non-interview settings.

A few years ago, I was at a party, but I didn't want to be there. The business was not going well. I made three seasons of *Meet the Adebanjos*; we'd made sales all over the world and had some successful years, but the sales were starting to dry up. The pressure started to build on me as I had a young family I had to provide for, and I had no money coming in for the foreseeable future. But because I was in showbiz, I kept getting invited to all these successful, rich people's parties. At these parties, people would come up to me and say, "Andrew, how's it going? Oh my God, I've watched your show. It's so amazing. You must be making so much money. You must be a multimillionaire. Well done." You can imagine the depression I must have felt, having to plaster on a fake smile and pretend like I was making mad money, when in reality that couldn't be further from the truth.

But I couldn't say no to a party because of the experience I had when I went to the conference at Harvard — you never know who you might meet. At one particular party, which was in a fancy apartment in Docklands, London, I bumped into a guy who said, "Hey, how are you doing, mate? My name is Bruce." I said, "Hey, my name's Andrew," and we got to talking. He told me he had just started up a film production company and he came from a background similar to mine; he was leaving a career in finance to pursue his dream of making movies. He asked me "Andrew, what would you do if you were in my shoes?"

Because of my experiences and how tough my life currently was, my first instincts were to tell him, "Don't do it. Do not do it. Forget about it; don't waste your time and your money." Also, the last thing I wanted to do is go to a party and discuss the film-making business. But I remember a saying that someone told me at the start of my TV production career: "You have to give some to get some." So, I concentrated on being positive, and, over the next hour, I focused on giving. I gave him advice from as much of my experience as possible. I answered any questions he had about how his business could work and thrive. I wasn't worried about giving away my secrets. I gave, gave, gave. At the end, he said, "Do you have a business card?" I did not have anything, so he said, "Let me take a number."

The next day, I got a phone call. He said, "Mate, all the advice you gave, I couldn't stop thinking about it all night. Can we meet up for coffee?" I went and met him for coffee, and he asked me more questions and I gave him even more advice. Two weeks later, he called me out of the blue again and said, "Look, I've been discussing with the team, and we need someone like you on board." And I was like, "I'm running my own production company. I'm busy," even though I wasn't that busy and I was dead broke. (I learnt many years ago that when it comes to negotiating, you have to look like you are unavailable so someone will want you more. 😊) He said, "Don't worry, we can pay you decent money to come on part-time as a consultant. Would you be willing to do two or three days a week?"

All because I went to a party I wasn't even excited about going to, I was able to get a paying job that kept me from going bankrupt. All because I gave something. Sometimes in life, you don't even realise when you're selling yourself, but if you're giving value, if you're offering solutions, if you're helping others, that can be enough to make people automatically see the need for you to be on their team. By giving, giving, giving, you will stand out and people will choose you. So, keep giving value and keep helping people; you'll be surprised how far that will go towards helping someone choose the 'why' in you.

ACTION POINT — HOW TO BE A NETWORKING MACHINE

Networking events are a perfect time to build rapport and stand out for potential employers. What is your mindset when you go to a networking event? You need to go with a mindset of impressing someone who might be able to help you with your internship goal.

Networking tips —

1. Come with memorable short stories. People remember stories, so come ready to impress.
2. Be a great listener — people give clues about themselves when they talk about themselves. So, listen intently and respond to what they say.
3. Be a problem solver; if someone tells you they have an issue or problem with anything, try to give them a solution. It doesn't matter if it's letting someone know how to cook a sponge cake better or telling people about the best clubs in Miami. Solve problems and you will be remembered.
4. Work on your small talk so that you don't bore anyone when you're speaking.

I NEED MONEY – FAST!!!!

I'd done all the hard work. I convinced the biggest TV station in Africa to take on a new series of *Meet the Adebanjos*. Debra and I were ecstatic – we had done the impossible – but there was one slight problem. They were only going to pay the money after we completed the show, which meant we wouldn't have any money to pay all the actors, production staff, production kit, venues, etc. during the production. We couldn't just tell the people who were going to be part of the production that they would have to wait 6 months before they got paid. So, this meant we needed to get a loan of hundreds of thousands of pounds to cover the shortfall. Wow. All this work, and I still have to go out there and find money.

Because we already had a signed contract from the TV stations saying they would pay us when we delivered the episodes, I thought it would be easy to get a loan from a bank. So, I told the team to press ahead with the preparations with the little money we had.

We got the studio in place and started to buy props and build sets and organise plans for the start of production. However, when I went to the banks, all UK banks refused because the TV station we were dealing with was not a UK TV Station.

I was on the verge of having to shut down the production, and I started to panic. I went to friends and current investors, begging them to give us money. "Please, please could you lend me money to get the show produced? We have come so far. We are so close. Please could you lend us the money?"

And no one budged. People said they would 'take their time to think about it' and didn't pick up the phone when I would chase them. Others said they had never done anything like this and didn't want to commit until we had more people. I needed the money fast.

Finally, I got one of my good friends on the phone and I explained to him the situation I was faced with. He said, "OK. Why should I lend you the money?" I said, "Because you are my friend and I will pay you back." He started to laugh. "Andrew, I can see why you are struggling to raise money." And then he proceeded to give me some great words of advice. He said, "You need to be able to structure your points and have more than one point. Sometimes people may have different things that will trigger their interest. And if you only give one reason why someone should lend you money, then you may be missing the reason that they're looking for."

He then went on to add, "You haven't addressed a key reason why people may be scared to lend you money — the risk factor! People will be scared of the risk of what happens if something goes wrong and you're not able to finish the production. Or if that African TV station decides to pull out and not pay you your money, what will happen?"

He was 100% correct. I hadn't structured my points effectively and hadn't explained how I would pay people back if anything went wrong. He ended by saying, "Use the rule of 3. Give three solid points on why someone should lend you money and clearly explain the points."

That night, I spent five hours refining my "Why Lend Me Money" story. The next morning, I called up an investor, and they asked, "Andrew, why should I lend you the money?"

I replied confidently, "You should lend us the money for three main reasons. The first reason is that to account for the risk of this loan, we will pay you 20% per annum on the money you lend. Secondly, if for any reason there is a disruption that causes the production to stop or the African TV company doesn't pay us, your loan will be guaranteed against the assets of the company, which are our current episodes we have. And, if worse comes to worst, we will sell our assets to pay you back your loan. Lastly, if you lend us over a certain amount I will put your name in as an executive producer on the show."

The investor went silent for what seemed an eternity and then said, "Send me the paperwork and I will send you the money today." Within 24 hours we raised enough money for the production to continue; all because I structured my 'Why Invest' into 3 clear points.

And we were true to our word. We paid the investors interest and we made a great production, which was paid by the African TV company. Everyone was happy!

ACTION POINT – STRUCTURE USING THE RULE OF THREE

Go back and look at your 'why you' sales pitch.

- Is it structured into 3 clear points?
- Do you provide clear, concise evidence to back up your points?
- Does it address any concerns the employer might have?
- Does it have a conclusion which iterates your message?
- Is it less than 60 seconds long?

COMMON "WHY YOU" INTERVIEW QUESTIONS

Use all you have learnt in this chapter to answer the following "why you" questions:

- Why should we hire you?
- How do you stand out from your peers?
- What is your greatest achievement?
- Can you sell yourself in 60 seconds or less?
- What do you see yourself contributing to this organization, in both the short- and long-term?
- How would colleagues describe you?

CHAPTER FIVE

PRACTICE, REVIEW, REPEAT

ANDREW OSAYEMI

BACK TO THE SCENE OF MY BIGGEST REJECTION!

So, you've researched. You've worked on your ideas. You are now not afraid to talk about how interesting you are. You've backed up your skills with examples. Now you need to put it all together and practise, get feedback, practise, get feedback, and repeat until you get your dream internship!

I'd learnt everything I could from Kay about what I needed to do to get a girlfriend. I'd worked on my chat-up lines, worked on my clothes so I could make a better impression, made sure I smelt better and always sported a fresh haircut. Now it was time to practise; to put it all to work and see whether or not I was able to use what I'd learnt, to try and get girls' numbers.

I went to Kay and proposed, "Look, we need to find somewhere where women are abundant so I can practise all I have learnt." He said, "I have the perfect place. We need to go back to Oxford Street." For those of you who don't live in London, Oxford Street is the shopping capital of the UK. It's jam-packed with people bustling in every hour — from plain old tourists to people who are into fashion, who want to either spend money or just hang out and have a good time. Oxford Street was also the scene of my biggest rejections. Kay was right — we needed to go to Oxford Street.

Kay's plan involved our going down to Oxford Street and just walking up and down the street, to practise talking to girls and try out whether the techniques I had learnt really worked.

The first day I went with Kay, every girl I spoke to said 'No' when I asked for her phone number. I was dejected and was terribly angry at Kay. I complained, "Kay, you made me spend all this money on a new hair cut and new clothes; made me spend countless hours practicing stories that would make me interesting and learn how to sell myself. And all for nothing! Not even one girl wanted to give me their number. Everything you have taught me is rubbish!!!"

Kay smiled and said, "Calm down, Andrew! Do you think when I first started going to Oxford Street I had any success? I went home crying even worse than you. Some of my rejections were so bad that I was too scared to even have eye contact with a girl for weeks. But I kept going back and I got better. You have to put in the work. You have to practise. Don't focus on the 'No' — focus on earning the 'Yes'!!

So, we went back to Oxford Street. Weekend after weekend. In the cold, in the rain and in the snow. I started to get used to being rejected and it started to hurt less and less. I was able to hone my skills, and I started to get better and better and better. I was also desperate for feedback, so even after a girl would reject me, I would sometimes ask what I could have done better. That would surprise the hell out of the girl because no rejected guy asks that. And because they were so surprised about me asking for feedback, they would tell me where I went wrong and even wish me good luck!!! Very soon, my rejection rate went from the 100% who would not give me any time of day to 80%. Then 70%. Then 50%. Now, for every two girls I was approaching, one was giving me her number. All because of practise and feedback and more practise!

You must be prepared to put in the work if you want to get your dream internship.

ACTION POINT — FIND PLACES TO PRACTISE

Have you found a place where you can practise all the things you need to work on and someone to help you? It could be a particular friend that you rehearse storytelling with, a meetup/society to provide you public speaking practise, or networking events to build up your networking. You need to find a place to practise what you've learnt.

Task: Identify three places/people you can use as your practise ground to try out your new skills.

SPEAKING AT MY MUM'S CHURCH

I remember it like it was yesterday. My mum had invited me to speak at her church. "Andrew, loads of people in the church love your TV show. Please, please come and talk about it at our business and entrepreneurship day." She pleaded. I reluctantly agreed. Deep down I didn't want to do it because I was scared of public speaking, but I didn't want to let my mum down. Normally I could just wing it when it came to public speaking, so I cast away my fears and committed myself to do this.

On the day of my talk, my mum was so excited as my dad drove us all to the church. When we got there, the place was packed – standing room only – with over 300 church members, most of whom had known me from when I was a baby. Their faces were so expectant when one of the ministers invited me to come up and speak.

The mood in the car on the way back home was completely different than the way it had been when we set off in the morning. It was full of silence. I had bombed the speech. I'd gotten on stage and struggled to communicate with the audience, I struggled to speak and didn't connect at all. Sometimes they say the hardest crowd to speak in front of is people you know; those that are close to you. And all through my speech, I could feel my mum's eyes burning on me from the back of the room as I was bombing on stage, just filled with embarrassment. Trying to break the silence in the car, I asked Mom, "How did that go? How did I do? I wasn't that bad, was I?" She just shook her head.

My dad said, "Son, you've *really* got to improve your public speaking."

That is when it hit me: I did need to do something about improving my public speaking. I don't know where you are, or what situation you're going through, but there's going to be an interview or an instance in your life that you will bomb so badly that you're forced to make a decision — either you quit or you knuckle down and work on getting better. It's happened to many great people in the past; before they reached their greatest achievement, they had to overcome their most abject failure. One example is the world-famous basketball player, Michael Jordan, who, after not even making the basketball team one year in high school, decided to train all through summer — and the rest is history.

At that point, I tried to focus on something that I'd been putting off for so long. I promised myself, *I'm going to improve my public speaking*. And at the beginning of the year, armed with my New Year's resolution, I walked into my first Toastmasters club, based in Croydon and called Speakers of Croydon.

Toastmasters is a speaking club open to the public, where people meet weekly to practise their public speaking. There are between 20 and 40 people in the audience and you can speak on any subject you want for about 5 to 7 minutes. After you finish, you are given tips on how you can improve your public speaking. It is a warm, friendly environment where you are surrounded by people who are committed to helping you improve your speaking. The meetings for Speakers of Croydon were every two weeks, and for the first six months, I never missed a meeting.

All of a sudden, my confidence got better. I improved in how I spoke, how I structured my speeches, the stories I told, the way I moved on stage — all because of practise. People started to look forward to when I was going to speak. One year after joining Toastmasters, I stood on stage in front of over 500 people at the finals of the Toastmasters UK Championship of Public Speaking. I spoke from my heart; I made people laugh, I made people cry, and I made people want more. My speech had an impact, so much so that I was placed second in the UK for public speaking (and that was even with my microphone cutting out at the start of my speech). See, success was there all the time, waiting. The talent was inside of me, but I needed to get coaching and to put in the work for it to come out.

You have talent, you have potential. It's just time for you to go back to basics and start putting in the work!! You need to be able to find an avenue or an arena where you can practise. You've got to be able to work, work, work. It's not going to be easy, but you've got to put in the work and practise.

ACTION POINT — JOIN A PUBLIC SPEAKING CLUB

How comfortable do you feel when speaking in public? Have you ever had any training? Find a local/online club where you can practise your public speaking. Even if you think you are good, you will learn how to get better. Toastmasters is a speaking club that I can recommend from personal experience, and the price of a meeting is cheaper than the cost of a coffee. But there are many speaking clubs out there. What you need is a place where every two weeks you can practise your technique.

- Find a public speaking club to join. Make sure you attend every meeting for at least the next six months.

LEFT ALONE MANAGING BILLIONS OF POUNDS

After the year when I went through 'Hunger Games' in my graduate job, I finally secured a full-time analyst position, as I mentioned in the previous chapter. Life was GOOD!

A month into being in the team full time, the managers, who believed in me and gave me my opportunity, were looking at me thinking, *Have we made a mistake?* You know that feeling you get when people believe in you and you feel like you're letting them down? I was in a high-paid, high-pressure position. The role I had was managing billions of pounds worth of transactions between different banks each day. Our job on the desk was to make money for our clients. And because there was so much to learn and because the work kept getting increasingly complex, I was struggling and making too many silly mistakes.

One day the boss left me in charge so he could go to the gym just for an hour during lunchtime. As he was leaving, he repeated, "Andrew, whatever you do, do not lose the desk money. Use the team pricing spreadsheet to quote prices for anyone who wants to buy EURUSD forwards." (EURUSD forwards allow firms to fix a EURUSD currency price for the future, and the price is constantly moving, depending on what the current financial market conditions are doing.)

I was super-diligent, and every second I checked to make sure the spreadsheets were running smoothly. And then, all of a sudden, I started to get inquiries from currency brokers (middlemen who buy and sell currency forwards for firms) looking for prices. I double-checked the spreadsheet and made sure our prices were in line and I started quoting prices. All of a sudden, the brokers were hitting my prices. (To hit a price in financial markets means someone was making an order based on a price I quoted and which I had to honour.) More and more brokers were calling to make orders. People were also making orders online since our spreadsheet controlled our online orders as well. Based on the spreadsheet, it looked like all these orders had made the desk money and I was happy. This was my chance to redeem myself after a month of making mistakes.

When the boss came back, I showed him, "Look, boss. I made so many orders. I've made the desk money." My boss looked at the order prices and was like, "Man, these order prices are wrong. All these trades have cost us money." I double-checked my spreadsheet. I was like, "No, no. Look at my spreadsheet— it says these prices were correct." The boss came over and looked at the spreadsheet, and said, "Look, fool. You had the pause button on. You can't pause a live spreadsheet."

When he pressed 'play' on my spreadsheet, it refreshed instantaneously, and I saw all the prices that I had quoted were wrong. This was the reason why so many people wanted to trade with me — I was giving them too good of a price! This meant we were losing money on each transaction!

That day we lost £30,000. The look the members of the team gave me was like, "Dude, you're not going to last long here." I knew I had to make a change. I knew I wasn't at my best. One reason was that the job started at 7:00 and finished at 18:00, which meant I had to get up at 5:30 am each day and I was too tired to put in extra work to improve and get up to speed. I didn't have enough time to practise getting better. I decided that I needed to find free time. So, starting that weekend I decided to come in on a Saturday and Sunday. As I walked into the office that weekend, I was surprised. I saw people there;

people that didn't need to be there. These were not just any people. These were all the top performers!

They also were putting in work on a Saturday and Sunday; at a time when the financial markets were closed, so they could catch up and work on strategies for the following week. This is what made them great and kept them as top performers. I started coming in on weekends to catch up and to get up to speed. Before long, *I* was one of the top performers. This was how I was selected to go to New York, within just two years at the bank, to be the head of the EURUSD forward desk in New York.

You've got to put in that work.

ACTION POINT — HOW MANY HOURS ARE YOU PRACTISING EACH WEEK?

How many hours are you putting in per week in pursuit of your dream? You need to be putting in at least one hour a day, practicing and getting better at your interview skills.

- Create a weekly training schedule on Sunday night each week. Plan your practise sessions for the week and stick to them, and you will start to see great improvements!

FIRING THE WHOLE CAST

We had done the impossible. We had finally secured over £100,000 from investors, which was enough for us to produce the first season of *Meet the Adebanjos*. All because of the hype from the pilot we had put on YouTube and the belief in me the investors gained!!

However, the money came with strings attached. The investors said, "We will only give you the money if you agree to make drastic changes and radical improvements for the upcoming season."

"What type of changes?" I asked.

"We want you to replace the entire cast!"

At first, I was offended. "What? Can't you see the response from the pilot?"

I spoke to Debra. "These guys don't get it. We need to find other investors; investors who believe enough in what we already have."

Debra pulled me back from my rant and said, "Andrew, let's be honest with ourselves. Let's actually watch the pilot again and see if the investors have a point about the cast."

We sat down and watched it, and as we watched it, we started seeing so many mistakes and so many things that could have been better. Deep down, we knew it was because we had rushed everything. We hadn't practised anything with the cast. We had come up with an idea, decided to make the show without first having much experience, and hadn't scrutinized the scripts. We just rushed into production. And even though we were lucky that what we produced had caused a great impact, we knew this wasn't our best work. This wasn't even up to 50% of our best work.

"What are we going to do?" I whispered to Debra.

Debra said, "We need to start again; to go back to basics and make sure that we do enough work and practise before we produce anything!"

We gathered all the cast from the pilot and pulled them together for dinner at Nandos. In hindsight, it probably was not the best thing to do over dinner because they came to the dinner all excited, thinking it was a celebration to announce that, because of the investors' money, they were going to be the new cast members of the new season. In fact, I had to look them all in the eye and say, "Unfortunately, this is the end of the road. We are going to have to start again with the show. We're going to have to re-cast the whole show."

Can you imagine telling all the cast members – who believed in your vision and came along with you for your pilot without getting paid much money at all – that after having raised the investment, we were going to scrap them and start again? It was one of the toughest things I have had to do in my life.

However, in your pursuit of perfection, in your pursuit of greatness, in your pursuit of achieving your goal in that dream internship, you're going to have to tear down some of the ideas that you've held on to for a long time. You're going to have to make sacrifices. You're going to have to upset some people. You're going to get a lot of push back from haters who say, "Why are you spending so much time looking for an internship? Why are you spending so much time on your interview skills? Why are you spending so much effort to gain new experiences by joining these societies and making new friends by networking?"

You're going to have to make sacrifices and you're going to have to make hard decisions. And that's what we had to do. We had to get rid of the whole cast. (Interesting fact: within that original cast was someone who would go on to become much bigger than our show. And that was Big Shaq, a.k.a. Michael Dapaah.)

But we had to do what we had to do. Sometimes you have to make sacrifices for your future. There's a famous saying that says: *What got you here won't get you there.* After all of those things that you've done to get you to this point in your life, you need to think to yourself, *What more can I do to get to the next level? How much more practise can I put in? How much more work can I put in?*

Debra and I decided to go back to basics. We hired new writers and a new cast. We did more research in learning the science and art of sitcoms. We reviewed sitcom writing and production courses just to learn, made sure the cast had time to practise the scripts. We did more script reads so we could make improvements if need be. And the result was that the new season was ten times better than the pilot, and it got an even better and bigger response from the public.

Are you ready to make sacrifices and put in the work?

ACTION POINT — RECORD YOURSELF ANSWERING INTERVIEW QUESTIONS

Are you video recording your mock interviews? A famous quote is: "Only things that are recorded can be measured". We were able to make changes because we went back and watched the pilot and unearthed things that had to be improved. You need to record yourself answering questions in a professional manner and send it to a person you can trust to give you feedback on what you can do to improve. Do you have someone who is giving you critical feedback on your interview skills? You need someone who can be critical and give you all the pointers on where you need to improve. It could be someone who has been successful at a job in the industry you want or an interview coach at university or a career help service. It could mean hiring a professional interview coach. Whoever you choose, ask for their most critical feedback so you can tear down all your bad habits and work on rebuilding the new and successful you.

- Start recording yourself answering interview questions. Find someone to critique your current interview performance and work on all the things they suggest. Get a check-up every month to see how you are improving.

GROWING UP IN THE GHETTO

I grew up in a deprived part of London; in public housing with multiple flats in a big block, which in the UK we call a council estate. In this council estate were so many different types of people — lower working class, immigrants, people on benefits, druggies, etc. But the number one thing that was rife in my council estate was gang violence. I remember walking home from school with my mom and asking her, "Why is there so much ketchup on the floor?" And she would say to me, "That's not ketchup, that's blood," while pulling me closer to her. We would see that on a regular basis. Lifts that were pissed in. Dirty and dark alleyways filled with weed smoke. My mum even had her handbag robbed multiple times!

However, I loved living there. I loved it because of the people and sense of community. I had so many friends on all the different floors of the council estate. You could knock on people's doors and find friends who would come out to play.

My mom was worried that I was going down a bad path. I remember at school I was always a popular person, always hanging out with a big group of friends. I was the joker; the trickster always doing a prank on teachers or friends. And this always made me get into trouble. One day, my mom got called to come to the school. You know that feeling you have when your mom is being summoned to your school? She was pissed. It was the early 90s, so I got licks the night before because she knew that anytime she got called to the school it was for something bad.

The next day, she turned up with me at the school, dragging me into the teacher's office. The teacher, who was my arch-nemesis, came in and sat us down.

"Mrs. Osayemi, I'm so happy you are here today."

My mom said in her thick Nigerian accent, "What? Why would you be happy when my son has done something wrong?"

"No, no, no. He hasn't done anything wrong. The reason I brought you in today is that your son got the highest mark in the area in the national maths test."

The teacher then said the following words, which changed my life. "Your son has potential. He just needs to make it count."

What my teacher said to my mum that day lit a fire under my mom. Sometimes in life, other people will discover the potential in you that you and your family didn't even know you had. It could be your teacher, coach, distant relative, mentor, etc. And if they can see it, other people can see it too.

Because of what my teacher said, my mom saw something in me — that I wasn't just a naughty kid. I was someone who, if I put my mind to it, could really achieve something. So, she started to push me. The first thing she did was find out through a family friend about social mobility schemes that helped anyone who came from a lower-income background to get into private schools for free. These schemes would pay your school fees, transport you to and from school, and cover your school uniform, school dinners, etc.

The scheme was perfect for anyone like me from a lower-income background, who couldn't afford private school. The only problem was that you would have to score one of the highest marks in the entrance exam to get considered. My mom said, "Look, no more playing out with your friends. It's time to work." And for two years she pushed me. Pushed me to work. Even found me a tutor who pushed me further. It was all about instilling a strong work ethic.

Sometimes we're a bit lazy. Sometimes we need a coach. Sometimes we need someone to believe in us. But that person can do only so much. You must do the work, but to do the work you need motivation.

At the start, I was rebelling against my mum telling me to work; that was her vision and not mine. But one day, one of my uncles took me for a drive. We drove past some beautiful buildings and manicured fields with football pitches, basketball and tennis courts, and swimming pools. I was like, "Wow! Uncle, these buildings and grounds are beautiful. I would love to one day be surrounded by a place like this." He agreed, "Oh yeah, these are the buildings and fields of the private schools your mum is telling you to work hard to get into. If you want to get into there, you need to put in the work."

I began to dream; to see myself in the school uniform, playing football in those fields. I started to visualise myself being there! I realized that I needed to do the work if I was going to make my dreams a reality. That was my motivation, and that's what I did. In the end, through my mom's hard work, determination and pushing, and my commitment to that work, I was able to get two fully paid scholarship offers to two private schools.

The reason you've picked up this book could be because someone has identified in you, or you've identified in yourself, that you have potential. Now, the next step is to put in the work. Are you ready to put in the work?

ACTION POINT — TIME TO VISUALISE SUCCESS

Have you visualised yourself actually being in your ideal job? You need to start believing you have what it takes and seeing yourself in the role.

- Go to the part of town where many firms in your industry are located. Walk around at lunchtime and get a sense of the people who work there so that you can start to see yourself as their equal. Also, go to the firm's lobby and visualize yourself going into work each day.
- Next, go home and increase the amount of work you are doing to achieve your goal!

WORKING WITH A YOUTUBE AND TV STAR!

A few years ago, I was lucky to have the privilege to work with an extremely popular online comedy influencer and TV actor. His name was Tolulope Ogunmefun and he was known online as Don't Jealous Me. He had transitioned from just being an online star to being a great TV actor, acting in *Sick Note* and *Man Like Mobeen.* I'd known him for many years, gave him his first TV role in my TV show, *Meet the Adebanjos*, and helped him create his own show, the *T-Boy Show*. So, we had a mutual trust and respect for each other. I think, in fact, he looked up to me in terms of someone that could provide guidance.

One day he came to me, asking if I had any ideas about projects he could do next. He wanted to branch out from just being an entertainer online and in TV shows. We went to a restaurant near his house and started to brainstorm. Suddenly out of the blue, both of us said, "What about a children's book?" You know how it feels when that light bulb moment hits? We both looked at each other and said, "That is it!!" He had just become the father of a baby girl, so doing a children's book made a lot of sense!

However, we had two big problems. First, neither of us had ever written or produced a book before, so we didn't even know what it took to publish a children's book. Secondly, we were already into October and we wanted people to buy the book for Christmas, which meant we had four to six weeks to get the book on the market.

We made the mistake a lot of people make when faced with challenging odds: we started randomly asking the opinions of others. Everyone said it couldn't be done. "You guys are crazy. Why the rush? Why don't you try to get a book deal with a publisher? Do you know it takes at least six months to get illustrations done by an illustrator?"

I told Tolu, "This reminds me of what everyone told me before I made the *Meet the Adebanjos* pilot. Everyone said it couldn't be done. Let's prove everyone wrong and self-publish this book! Show everyone that, with hard work and determination, anything is possible." Luckily, Tolu was on the same wavelength as I was. He knew that if we waited another year, the momentum would die down and something else would take over. He declared, "Let's prove these haters wrong!"

I'm a big believer in momentum when it comes to goals and ideas. If you want to do something, you have to do as much possible while you have the drive. You want to be so deep into what you are doing before the momentum dies that you are forced to keep going. For example, if you are trying to lose weight, you want to do as much as possible in the first month to set you up for the rest of the year. If you don't drive yourself in that first month, it will be easier to give up as soon as you lose interest.

Also, you have to be careful of people putting limits on you. People will always come up with these so-called rules to try and put you in a box. Your job is to always have the vision of something bigger and better; something not confined in any box.

Once you have that commitment – once you have that belief – you can achieve way more than you ever thought was possible.

Within a week we had the first draft of the book done. We wrote it by going back and forth on WhatsApp! Within two weeks, we had gotten illustrators to sketch up all the pages. Within three weeks, we had found a book printer who could print the book at a cost-effective price. And within five weeks we had the finished copy of the book —*The Frog and His Dancing Shoes*. All because of that vision and our refusal to allow anybody to tell us we couldn't make it happen.

That Christmas we sold over 1000 copies. After Christmas, Tolu called me and said, "I think we could go bigger. Let's make this a live experience at schools, with an actual dancing frog." I agreed, "Let's do it!"

What did the haters tell us? "Are you crazy? You don't have the right clearance to get into the schools. No one's school is going to let you in."

We knew enough not to listen to the 'nay-sayers' and decided once again to challenge the status quo. We started emailing hundreds and hundreds of schools across the UK every day, asking if we could come in and entertain their kids with a live show.

Most (99%!) of the schools didn't reply but 1% did and said they would love to have us. This allowed us to create a book tour, visit the classrooms and promote the book *The Frog and His Dancing Shoes* in schools. This allowed us to sell out all the copies of the book we had self-published.

Don't let other people's limitations put boundaries on you and your ambitions! Prove them wrong by working hard.

ACTION POINT — SCREW THE HATERS

In life, you are going to have haters — people who tell you can't do something. They will attempt to put roadblocks in front of you. Your mission is to focus on the end goal and drown out the sound of all those haters.

- Write down every message and comment that a hater has said to you about your goal. Print them, read them and then rip them up!! Use this as your motivation and the fuel you need to hit your end goal!!

GET OR CREATE A MENTOR

Do you remember my telling you at the beginning of this book how bad I was on my first investment banking interview? After that experience, I almost quit in my pursuit of getting into investment banking.

This is why it's good to surround yourself with positive people who are accomplishing things at a higher level than yours. Luckily for me, my university housemate, Magatte, was that type of person. He was already crushing it with investment bank interviews. In fact, he already had three or four banks that were begging him to come and do an internship there. He told me, "Andrew, you've got what it takes." I said, "No, I haven't." He insisted, "Look, I've spent six months living with you, and I know you. Trust me, you have what it takes; you just need to work on getting interview-ready."

Again, as they did earlier, someone saw talent in me that I didn't believe I had.

I said, "Well, I don't know what to do."

"Look, let me give you help."

And he sat down with me and started to coach me on the things I needed to learn — the websites I needed to be reading, the technical information I needed to be studying, the types of maths, the calculations and everything. He did mock interviews with me. All because, again, he saw the potential I had. And I started to get better and better and better. He even offered me a technique for applying to as many internships as possible, even the internships you don't want, just to get an interview. This was designed to give me a chance to practise in a professional environment so that I wouldn't be intimidated by corporate surroundings. Doing this meant that by the time I got the chance to interview for an investment banking position I genuinely wanted, I was prepared and I was ready. This led to my getting a summer internship, which completely changed my life and launched my career in investment banking.

You need to find someone in your circle who has done better than you or look elsewhere for people who have done better than you. Who you can ask for guidance or tips? Some of us are not lucky enough to have someone like that. This means you have to create your own virtual mentor/guru. When I first started in TV, I wasn't fortunate to have someone I could speak with. So, what did I do? Google became my mentor! I found podcasts on TV, found blogs on TV, joined online forums about TV and even found online courses about how to make money in TV.

Never make the fact you don't know anyone in a particular industry an excuse for your not being successful. Use Google, obtain as much knowledge as possible, pay for some courses. People always say they don't have money for courses, but these days there are courses for every budget. So, don't use money as an excuse. In fact, ditch *all* the excuses and go after your goal!!

ACTION POINT — APPLY TO EVERYTHING TO GET INTERVIEW PRACTISE

Sometimes your biggest obstacle is lack of actual interview practise. Therefore, you should apply for work that you are overqualified for – jobs you know you will be called to interview for – just to get real-life interview practise. You know you don't want the job, but this is to get genuine experience! It doesn't matter what the job is, you just want the practise. You want to experience the pressure of waking up, putting on your smart clothes − your business clothes − and getting to the appointment on time. Being there in reception and waiting to be ushered in. Having that nervous energy, trying to build rapport. Trying to get another person to laugh and to like you is all about practise.

- Apply to five easier, less desirable jobs today, so that you can line up practise interviews.

AFTERWORD

So, you've made it to the end of the book. And I know you're probably thinking, *There's a lot of great advice here, but does this actually work?* I'm here to tell you — it does. I have helped thousands and thousands of people like you get top internships at major global firms by using these methods. So, it does work, but you've got to put in the effort!!!

"No, Andrew, I wasn't talking about it working for me getting an internship—I know it will help me. I want to know if your advice helped you get a girlfriend!"

That is a personal question I get asked a lot 😊.

After soaking up all the advice from Kay and improving my success rate of getting a phone number from a girl I liked to 50% (a big first step), let's just say my love life went from non-existent to amazing. But I was still not able to find the love of my life. Then one night I walked into a club and saw someone that took my breath away; someone I knew instantly was my soulmate. But I was nervous. I didn't know what to do or how to approach her. Suddenly, Kay's words came back to me.

"The first thing is, do your research and find out what, what, what, she's into." But how I could that, in a noisy club, if I don't even know her? Then I thought the best research I could do is just wait around and see what song she gets up and dances to. When that song comes on, then I can move in and dance with her and sweep her away! So, I sat there patiently waiting. Hours passed by until, towards the end of the night, her favourite song came on and she jumped up, excited, and started to dance.

That's it, this is my moment, I thought. I was ready to make my move, ready to go in. But all of a sudden, someone else beat me to the chase and started dancing with her. I said to myself, *Oh my God, what am I going to do next?* And then I remembered another piece of Kay's advice: *You've got to prove it.* So, undeterred, I moved up next to the man dancing with my future soulmate and I danced my heart out!! All my dancing practice began to show and all of a sudden there was a big circle around me, and people started shouting "Go, Andrew, Go Andrew". I just kept dancing more energetically. This caught the attention of the girl I was so attracted to. She stopped dancing with my arch-nemesis and stood watching me dance. When the song stopped and the people applauded, I smoothly slid over to her and asked her if she wanted to dance.

Later, I asked her on a date, and on my way to meet her I had the voice of Kay in my ear: *Don't be boring. You have to be interesting!* On that date, I made her laugh so much, we connected over common interests! I had passed the test and very shortly she was my girlfriend.

Many years later, it was time to ask her the big question: Will you marry me?

I made sure I used Kay's advice of *Make sure you have perfected your 'why me' story.* I made sure I practised it and perfected it. I made sure it was complete and structured. And luckily, when I asked the big question, she said 'yes'.

So, I hope I have answered your concerns. Yes, this did help me with my love life, and it can help you also. But all joking aside, I know the main reason you picked up this book is that you wanted to get a dream internship.

All these secrets I have shared today have helped me throughout my life. They've helped me get a high-paying job working at an investment firm, helped me pivot and go into TV production and make a TV show that is now on Netflix, and helped me help thousands of people like you get an internship and ultimately their dream full-time job.

So, my challenge to you today is to go back and read this book again. Go through all the action points and, no matter what anyone may tell you, keep focused, keep working hard, keep improving yourself. You will succeed and get a top internship!

If this book has benefitted you in any way, please share it with your friends, because this is about giving back. This is about helping each other achieve the best things in life. This book will help you not just get your dream internship but also launch whatever dream idea you have. Remember friends, you can do it. You have potential. All you have to do is work hard!!

Good luck.

WANT MORE? Follow me on LinkedIn to hear more of my crazy stories and to get access to my exclusive interview help webinars https://www.linkedin.com/in/andrew-osayemi/

APPENDIX

Sample Interview for Any Top Internship

Interviewer: Hi, Andrew, thank you for coming to interview with us today. How is your day so far?

Thank you for having me. My day has been fantastic. I woke up early and went on my usual early morning run. I find running early revitalises me and gives me energy. I then got ready and made it down here in time, luckily avoiding the train delays on the central line!

Interviewer: Tell me about a time you had to solve a complex problem.

It was 4am and I had just finished a 3-hour epic DJ set at an event in Kingston. As I was walking to the car, out of nowhere a thug-looking guy ran up to me, pulled out a gun, pointed it at me and said, "Give me the money you made from DJing tonight."

You can imagine what was going through my mind at the time. *OMG, I'm going to die….. What will my parents think if I were to die in cold blood…?, Why was I so stupid to walk in the dark by myself…? Is that gun even real…?, Should I run or cry for help…?* My final thought was, *Is there any way I could plead and negotiate with this person?* So I said to him very calmly and very collected, "Look, I didn't make much money tonight. If you reach into my pocket you will find all I have." He took the money, but said, "This isn't much. Give me more." I was about to tell him again I didn't have anything more, but then I remembered I had a watch I loved and treasured. I quickly decided that if I gave it to him that would be enough for him to let me go. I gave him the watch. He looked at it, put it on and grinned, "That's what I'm talking about." And he looked around and just ran off.

By staying calm, by being collected, I was able to escape with my life, even though it cost me money and my watch. But I learned something very valuable from that situation. Being calm and thinking things through gives you the best chance to deal with stressful, complex situations. If I had freaked out and panicked, who knows what would have happened? But by staying calm and being composed, I was able to overcome the situation. That is a skill I have and one I would love to display at your company.

Interviewer: Tell me about a time you had to deal with a difficult team member.

I was the executive producer of a TV show, and we had a star actor who was a nightmare to deal with. No one liked him. He would berate the staff, shout at them, get angry, but then he'd go into his shell and become all emotional when he forgot his lines on set. It got so bad that some of our best production staff were considering quitting. I debated in my head the various things I should do to resolve the situation. *Should I replace the actor? But this actor was a big star! Or was it actually the staff's fault because they couldn't handle the actor?* At the end of the day, I resolved that team morale was more important than one superstar actor. I went to the actor and gave him an ultimatum. I said, "Look, if you don't change your ways, I'm going to have to replace you." He said, "No, you can't do that." So I told him,

"Watch me. We can write you out and we can start again." The actor looked in my eyes and could see I was serious.

After having that talk, the actor never behaved like that again, and the set was better for it. The morale was better. And in the end, when we finished filming, the actor came to me and thanked me. "Look," he said, "I was going through a lot. Thank you for putting me back on the straight and narrow. I feel a lot better for it."

So, what I learned from that situation is that fostering team morale is more important than trying to satisfy one individual. And if you're direct, if you're honest, if you deal with things head-on, you have a better chance of resolving it instead of just letting it fester. And if you hire me, I will bring that team spirit to this company.

Interviewer: Tell me about a time you failed at something.

Two years ago, I was told I needed to build my personal brand and I should post on LinkedIn some inspirational stories about my life. So, I made my first post, and my first ever post on LinkedIn got over 12,000 likes. 12,000! I thought I was the man. I thought, *Wow this is easy, I am now a LinkedIn influencer*. My next post on LinkedIn didn't get 13,000 likes but still got around 3000 likes. People started to message me. *Wow, Andrew, this isn't normal. You must have a gift for writing. You are going to be a major star on the platform.* I thought, *Finally, I'm going to be big.*

The following post got 30 likes. And the post after that got 10 likes. From 13,000 to 10 likes. People started to message me saying, *What happened? We haven't ever seen someone drop so many likes.* I felt like such a massive failure, heightened by the fact it was such a public humiliation. When I went back and analysed the post that got few likes, I realized something—I wasn't being myself in these posts. I started to write what I thought people would like instead of from my true voice. I wasn't being genuine about who I was.

The reason why I connected with so many people in the beginning, apart from that it truly was an inspirational story, was that it was genuine and written in my own voice and style. When I started copying the styles of others – trying to use writing gimmicks – I forgot my real voice and I lost the way I was coming across. I was no longer authentic. That day I resolved that, at the end of the day, it doesn't matter about the number of likes; all that matters is keeping your voice, keeping your point of view, because with that you can add value. And nowadays, whether or not I get loads of likes or no likes, all I'm focused on is being authentic and being true to my point of view.

Interviewer: What's your greatest weakness?

One of my greatest weaknesses, from early on in my career, was being intimidated when I was in situations where I didn't have much previous exposure. For example, when I started in banking and TV.

It was mainly because of my background—coming from social housing, growing up with so little, not having the right network, which always made me feel inferior to others, who had a better upbringing and came from a better social class. It made me feel intimidated and shy to speak up and show my true self. I had spoken to many people about how I could overcome this, and it was only after listening to podcast interviews of people who, I thought, came from a higher social class that I found out others had insecurities too. That they grew up 'trying to be normal and not so posh'. That life wasn't all rosy for them, and I got the feeling that some even envied the background and life that 'regular people' had. Their underlying message was that you have to be proud of where you come from and own it. Whether you come from a working-class, middle-class or upper-class background, you have to remind yourself that if you are in the room you deserve to be in the room. So be yourself! That gave me the confidence to be myself and not feel intimidated. With this new sense of confidence, I can assure you I will also be a bright and positive influence for everyone I work with.

Interviewer: What's one of the biggest risks you had to take in your life?

I once had to shut down a very expensive TV production, knowing the investors' money, the TV station's money, and everything was all on the line because the dad of one of our main actors was ill.

He wasn't just ill 10 miles, 20 miles, 100 miles, even a thousand miles away—he was ill about 3,000 miles away in Nigeria. One particular day at 5am, I get a phone call. I pick up and it's the main actor, "My dad is very ill; I need to go see him just in case anything happens." My first reaction is, *Oh my God.* In my head I'm thinking, *The production is ruined. If he goes and doesn't come back, that could end up costing us thousands, hundreds of thousands of pounds. But on the other hand, this is our main actor. If he's not able to see his dad, what happens? Will he quit the show and go anyway? If he does turn up, will his performance be the same?*

I was dumbfounded, not knowing what to say. But at that moment I remembered a principle my parents taught me growing up. If you take care of people, people will take care of you. If you give to others, someone will give back to you. So, I said, "Look, go. We'll shut down the production for a week, we'll get you a flight to Nigeria in the morning. But please, give me your word you're going to come back. Whatever happens, say you're going to come back." To this day, that actor's always grateful because he went there, he saw his dad, and connected with him on an emotional and spiritual level, in a way money could never buy, and he was able to come back. He kept his word and he came back. I'm not going to lie—during those seven days he was away, I couldn't sleep. Every day I was thinking, *Oh my God, I'm going to get a phone call telling me he's not coming back, which would mean we lose it all.*

But he did come back, and he gave us even greater performances; he took the show to bigger heights. What I learned from that is, your staff is everything in a job or a project. So, if you give as much as possible to your staff and make their lives easier, they will give back to you and do all they can to make your project a success.

Interviewer: You mentioned you are hardworking. Can you give me an example?

Imagine this. At the age of 22, I had two jobs. One was working at an investment bank as a trader, which meant I had to be up at 5:30 and at work by 7:00 each day. I would work flat out during the day, hardly getting up to grab a lunch because I had to be fixed on the screen and watching the markets. I finished work at 6:00 PM.

Then I had to go to my job of being a DJ, which meant having to get to the club by 10pm and finishing at 3am. You would think that I would only DJ on the weekends and work in the bank during the week, but sometimes I got booked for big university gigs during the week all over the country.

I remember one particular day when I finished work at the bank at 6pm and then rushed to jump on the train to Bristol, where I was going to DJ in front of a thousand people at university club. I had a little sleep on the train, got to the club at around 10pm, DJed until 3pm, then got back on the train to go straight back to London around 6am. Rushed to work and I was there at 7am, ready for another full-day shift

Even though I was working around the clock, my performance at both places was excellent. So, I can work hard, very hard, and I guarantee I will bring that same strong work ethic to your company. (And to reassure you, I don't DJ on the weeknights anymore LOL.)

Interviewer: You say you're good at sales. Can you expand on that and give me any examples?

Can you imagine? You spend over £100,000 of your investors' money to create a TV show and no-one wants to buy it in your home country? So, you have to travel around the world trying to get sales, not even knowing if people are interested. That was a situation I was faced with. I couldn't make the sale in the UK, then someone told me that there's an opportunity at a conference in Africa to meet people who may want to buy it. The conference was in Ghana, where I had never been before. I just went in, confident in my selling ability, and over the years I travelled to many countries. I didn't have any strong sales leads—I had to be able to make the sales on my own.

So, I think my greatest skill is being able to make sales when nothing is guaranteed. I can generate the lead, I can build interest, I can close the deal, and I can even chase down the money promised. I've been able to prove through my international work that I am good at sales. I've sold shows to over 30 countries and I've also been able to strike deals with some of the world's biggest companies, including Netflix, to generate revenue far in excess of the original £100,000 investment. I can't wait to start selling your company's products, and I promise I will sell them with the same vigour and passion I have always shown throughout my life.

Interviewer: How do you stand out from your peers?

In two ways: I have an entrepreneurial mind, but I also have a creative mind.

Most people will tell you that those two things don't mix. Either you get creatives, or you get entrepreneurs, but I'm here to tell you that I can get both.

My entrepreneurial experience stems from hustling since I was young, whether it was being a club promotor, making TV shows and selling them around the world, or helping other companies build their ideas or making their ideas flourish— I've done it and my track record proves itself.

But on the other hand, I'm also a creative. Not many people know that I was a co-writer on a TV show, writing over 50 episodes. I can sit down with a group of writers, a group of creators, and work and flourish and develop ideas. On LinkedIn I can sit down and write and craft stories that I know will make people laugh and take action.

I believe I can bring in both of these traits and add value to your organisation. I can help with the creativity side in terms of your branding and marketing, and I can also help with the selling, the business and execution. So, if you hire me, you'll get two for the price of one.

Interviewer: Why should we hire you?

First, my experience of taking ideas and converting them into well-loved brands. And secondly, my loyalty and willingness to make sacrifices. At the age of 27, I left a well-paying job and took the risk of a lifetime; I took an idea on paper and turned it into a TV show that has been watched by millions across the world. I can do the same for your company with any ideas you have—develop them, nurture them and make them into a worldwide success.

I'm also someone who is very loyal and will sacrifice a lot to get the job done. I left a well-paying job in banking to start the TV production company. For many years, the show didn't make any money. For many years, I lived off the bare minimum, but I stood with my team. I stood with my people. I've stood with the idea and ultimately led it to success. And I will do the same for your company. I will sacrifice for the team, I'll be loyal to the team, I'll be loyal to the company.

So, to conclude, you should hire me because of my experience of taking ideas from scratch and making them into worldwide successes. And for the assurance that I will be loyal and do whatever it takes to make your company a success!

Printed in Great Britain
by Amazon